MAKE YOUR OWN

AMAZING

YouTube

VIDEOS

BRETT JUILLY

MAKE YOUR OWN AMAZING YouTube VIDEOS

LEARN HOW TO FILM, EDIT, AND UPLOAD QUALITY VIDEOS TO YOUTUBE

FOR YOUNG READERS

Racehorse for Young Readers books may be purchased in bulk at special discounts for sales promotion, corporate gifts, fund-raising, or educational purposes. Special editions can also be created to specifications. For details, contact the Special Sales Department, Skyhorse Publishing, 307 West 36th Street, 11th Floor, New York, NY 10018 or info@ skyhorsepublishing.com.

Racehorse for Young Readers™ is a pending trademark of Skyhorse Publishing, Inc.®, a Delaware corporation.

Visit our website at www.skyhorsepublishing.com.

10 9 8 7 6 5 4 3 2 1

Library of Congress Cataloging-in-Publication Data is available on file.

Cover design by Michael Short
Cover photograph: [TK]
Interior photography: [TK]

ISBN: 978-1-63158-202-8
eISBN: 978-1-63158-207-3

Printed in China

TABLE OF CONTENTS

INTRODUCTION

People like you make all different kinds of videos on YouTube. There are cat videos and prank videos. Gaming videos, vlogs, and makeup tutorials. Serious news reports and celebrity gossip. How-to videos, reaction videos, music videos, and probably a hundred other kinds.

This book is going to focus on the simple formula that almost all videos use. With this formula, you can make vlogs, makeup tutorials, news shows, reactions, how-to videos, cooking videos, and so many more types. The formula has just two steps.

Step 1: Pick a topic.

Step 2: Talk about it, demonstrate it, or bring your viewers along with you while you do it.

Yes, most YouTube videos are that simple! You've probably watched dozens, hundreds, or even thousands of videos in which an enthusiastic YouTuber pops onscreen and says something like this:

You can make videos about almost anything!

- ❏ "Hey guys! I'm going to the beach today, and I'm taking you along with me."

- ❏ "Hi! I'm Emily, and I'm going to do a beginner makeup tutorial for you guys. It's a step-by-step of how to get this beautiful cat's eye look."

- ❏ "Welcome to News with Nicholas! I'm Nicholas, and today's top story is celebrities blowing money on

Popular YouTuber Luke Korns announcing his video, "I learned to play the guitar in 24 hours.

> expensive cars they don't need, and making the rest of us feel poor! Especially me, because I don't have a car!"

These YouTubers each picked a topic, then made a video about it. Just two steps.

But before you run off and grab your cell phone to start shooting, you should know there is actually a little more to it than that. You've probably also seen videos that start with someone awkwardly sitting in a dark room, mostly in shadow so you can't see them, mumbling about some topic that isn't very interesting. So even though that YouTuber had a topic and wanted to make a video about it, they didn't focus on making their video look or sound good, and they didn't pick a topic that anyone would be interested in.

That's what this book is about. You'll learn how to come up with interesting topics, then shoot and edit your videos so they look good, sound good, and are fun to watch. You'll learn about framing, lighting, cut scenes, intros, outros, metadata, and all the other "tricks of the trade" that the most popular YouTubers use.

YouTube is a lot of fun. Making good videos is easier than you think. Let's get started!

PART ONE:
THE BASICS

HOW TO COME UP WITH GREAT VIDEO IDEAS

Unless you're going to walk around shooting video twelve hours a day, you probably won't catch an amazing event on your phone that will go viral on YouTube. You'll need to plan topics for the videos you make.

All popular YouTubers do this. Even unpopular YouTubers do this. Luckily, it's not hard! And after you've been picking video topics for a while, you won't even have to think about it.

Start with Things You Love

The easiest videos to make are about topics you already love! So, what are your hobbies? Are you into one particular sport? Gymnastics? Martial arts? Do you really like drawing? Or coming up with short

> **PRO TIP:**
> Anything you enjoy doing or thinking about can be a great topic for videos!

stories? Are you a baker? Do you enjoy makeup? What about math, or programming, or inventing? How about tabletop games?

Think about what you and your friends talk about most. Is it a band? A video game? School? Dating? Clothes? Homework? Fast food? Bad jokes?

You can make videos out of any of those topics!

General Topics with Many Approaches

Now that you've narrowed it down to a few topics, consider how you might approach each one of them in different ways. Some topics have more options when it comes to your approach. For example, let's say you like soccer and you're going to start a soccer channel. In your videos, you could:

Kids playing soccer.

- ❑ Talk about your favorite team.
- ❑ Talk about your favorite players.
- ❑ Talk about moves you've learned. Demonstrate how to do them.
- ❑ If you are on a team, have someone shoot a video of you playing and make a "highlight" reel. (Or a blooper reel!)
- ❑ Talk about strategies you know, and show pictures of how everyone on the team should be positioned on the field, and why that formation is so effective.

Let's say you like doing makeup, so you're starting a makeup channel. You could make videos about:

If you apply it on the inner part only and blend it to the outer part to make gradation lip easily.
입술 안쪽에만 바르고, 손으로 바깥쪽까지 펴발라주면 감장히 쉽게 그라데이션 립이 완성됩니다.

A makeup tutorial from Owiena Tan.

- ❑ your morning makeup routine
- ❑ your nighttime skincare regimen
- ❑ product reviews
- ❑ "everyday makeup" tutorials
- ❑ Halloween makeup tutorials
- ❑ different looks and techniques
- ❑ how to recreate celebrity makeup looks
- ❑ comparing two different mascaras, two different lipsticks, etc.

Or you might be an up-and-coming chef or baker. You could have a cooking channel where you:

- ❑ Demonstrate how to cook dishes that you love.

- Show off cooking and food-preparation techniques.

- Talk about the culture of each of the dishes, or food techniques from different cities (Chicago pizza vs. New York pizza),

"Baking With Mimi & Marbles" from jasonrip99.

countries (France, China) and regions (Northern vs. Southern Italy).

- Try bizarre foods. Try combining foods that don't usually go together. Try a food you've always been scared to eat.

And everybody loves jokes, so let's say you're creating a comedy channel. Think of different ways to present your personal brand of humor:

- Get funny people in your videos. Make up jokes with them.

- Learn a new joke every day and make a video out of it.

- Write jokes of your own.

Me planting my face on my wife's foot, in my video about taking "face-palm" to the next level. (Because "face-foot" is more extreme than "face-palm"!)

- Ask your viewers to come up with jokes on a particular topic, like the latest viral video or celebrity news story, and read them in your next video.

If you want to think of even more angles for the topic you chose, subscribe to other YouTubers who talk about the same things as you.

When you watch their videos, notice the different things they talk about in that same topic. That will stimulate your imagination!

Long-Term Goal Videos

Another good topic for videos is a long-term goal. If you're working toward something like learning how to dance, getting fit, or becoming an actor, you could make videos with updates on your progress a few times a week. (That's a great basis for an entire YouTube channel. Think: "Laura's Fitness Channel!" or "Jared Learns to Skateboard.") Let's say you're getting in shape. You could:

> **YOUTUBE TALK**
> "Vlog" is short for "video blog" just like "blog" is short for "web log." A vlog is a casual video where you discuss a topic.

- ❏ Shoot a video about the different exercises you do.

- ❏ Record some of your workouts.

- ❏ Make regular updates about the progress you're making; I used to weigh X, now I weigh Y. I used to be able to lift this much, now I can lift this much. My waist was X inches, now it's Y.

- ❏ If you add a new exercise to your routine, make a video about it.

- ❏ Vlog about things that you learn along the way.

You don't have to be an expert to take this approach! When you start off and you're a newbie, viewers will like you because you're an underdog just learning how to do something. You'll probably attract viewers who will help you out and give you tips! Another major benefit is that long-term goals have a lot of steps, so that's a lot of videos you can make!

Trending Topics

You can find trending topics on YouTube, Twitter, Google, and lots of other sites. If you find a popular trending topic that you like, you might be able to make a video out of it easily.

Actually, you're already surrounded by trending topics. Just notice what

your friends talk about, what you see your favorite YouTubers talking about, what video ads appear before videos (if there are any), and if you watch TV, notice what commercials are running. (Yes, you should watch TV commercials if you're looking for trending topics!)

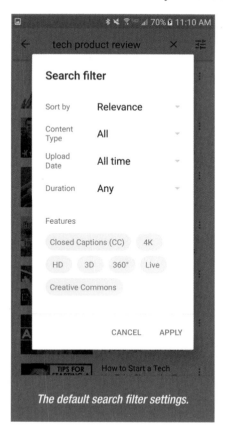

The default search filter settings.

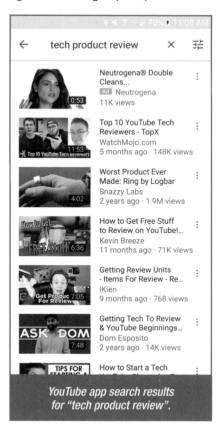

YouTube app search results for "tech product review".

YouTube has a feature that lets you see how popular a topic is. On a phone or tablet, in the YouTube app, type in a search term that matches the topic you picked. Then, on the upper right, there's an icon that looks like three horizontal sliders. Tap that, and you'll see the "Search filter" menu. In the drop-down for "Sort by," select "View count". That will make the most popular videos appear first in the results. In the "Upload Date" drop-down, select either "Today" or "This week." That will make the results only show recent videos. Tap "Apply" at the bottom of the screen. Then you can watch the most recent videos, and see what those people are saying about that topic.

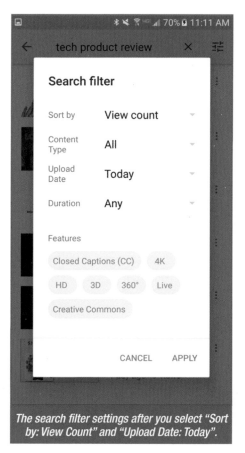

The search filter settings after you select "Sort by: View Count" and "Upload Date: Today".

The process is similar on a computer when you're viewing YouTube in a browser like Chrome or Firefox. Type in a search term and press enter. Then click on the "Filter" button in the upper left of the screen. In the filter menu, click on "Today" or "This week" in the left column. That will show recently uploaded videos only. Click the "Filter" button again, then click on "View count" in the right column. Your results will now show the most popular new videos at the top of the list.

Trending topics are popular and can get you a lot of views because people are searching for them. But be careful. People are only interested in those topics for a few days or a week, so your video could become a "tentpole" video instead of an "evergreen" video.

Tentpole Videos

A tentpole topic is great for getting a lot of views over a short period of time. Nearly every viral video falls into this category; it will spike in popularity for a few days or weeks, then a month later it's only getting a few views, and within three months nobody's watching it anymore.

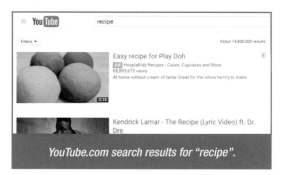

YouTube.com search results for "recipe".

Christmas is a tentpole topic; it's super-popular in December, but on December 26th, nobody's interested anymore.

Tentpole video topics are pretty easy to come up with. Just pick any new video game release, any celebrity scandal, any major world event, any music festival like Coachella or Lollapalooza, any convention like Comic-Con or VidCon or E3, and make a video about it. Your video will get a lot of views for a few days, and two weeks later your views will have dried up. It may sound as though it's impossible to make a successful channel if you upload tentpole videos. But there is a way to be successful: you need to upload tentpole videos frequently.

The Filter menu appears after you click on the "Filters" button in the upper right.

That's how "news" channels work. Philip DeFranco has done this for years. He uploads a video every weekday, talking about the latest, biggest news stories on the Internet. He gives simple summaries of the stories, gives his opinions and thoughts about what's going on, and then asks viewers to comment with their own opinions.

YOUTUBE TALK

"Tentpole" topics are popular for just a few weeks or days, and then they lose popularity. They are actually named after the poles that hold up a tent. The fabric top of the tent is held up by the tentpoles. But between the tentpoles, the fabric droops. Like your video views will in a few days time.)

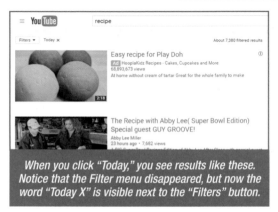

When you click "Today," you see results like these. Notice that the Filter menu disappeared, but now the word "Today X" is visible next to the "Filters" button.

Anyone searching for videos about those news stories will find Philip DeFranco's videos. However, no one is going to search for news stories from last month or last year, so Philip needs to upload regularly to keep getting views on his videos.

You can click on the "Filters" button again, when "Today" is already selected.

Evergreen Videos

An evergreen video will continue getting views for years and years. "How-to" videos are usually evergreen; a video about how to change a car tire will get views today, tomorrow, next year, and ten years from now. The process for changing a car tire is going to stay the same, and people will always need to know how to do it.

It's a little tougher to come up with evergreen videos than it is to come up with tentpole videos. One reason is that YouTube already has a lot of evergreen videos. If you want to make a video about how to teach your dog to sit, you'll probably find that there are thousands of videos about that topic already.

But if you can come up with a new evergreen topic, you'll get views for years. Some of my videos are like this. For example, I used to have a video called "How to Make Money if You're a Kid." It kept getting lots of views every month, because kids always want to know how to make money! YouTube removed it after a few years

> **YOUTUBE TALK**
> "Evergreen" videos are about topics that people will always search for, like how to do a backflip or how to keep a door hinge from squeaking. "Evergreen" videos are named after evergreen trees, trees that stay green all year, like pine, spruce, and redwood.

because I did some things I shouldn't have with the video description. You'll learn about that in the chapters on YouTube Metadata and the "Don't" list.

A Fun Way to Brainstorm

Whether you're still on the fence about a topic or you've picked one and want to decide how you'll approach it, take some time to brainstorm. For me, that means writing down a list of ideas. The great thing is that most of the ideas can be terrible! When you're brainstorming ideas on a topic, the goal is to come up with a LOT of ideas. The goal is to not filter yourself. The goal is to write down, type out, and say everything that comes to mind.

I usually tell myself to come up with ten ideas or more. I use this technique when I'm coming up with jokes for videos; I tell myself I have to write down at least ten things that might be funny about a topic, even if they're dumb, insensitive, or would only make sense to my friends.

The great thing about making yourself list at least ten ideas is that the first few ideas are easy, but the last few ideas really force you to think crazy. The process forces you to come up with ideas you never would have come up with if you were just trying to come up with one perfect idea or joke. And sometimes those last few ideas, the ones that are the most insane, are the best!

Your friends might be able to help too, especially friends who are creative. Make sure they know that you're trying to come up with as many ideas as possible, and not just one perfect idea. If they don't get that, they may get in the way of your brainstorming process. But if you let yourself get silly, and think of things you'd never think of otherwise, you can come up with some good video topics!

PRO TIP:
"The way to get good ideas is to get lots of ideas, and throw the bad ones away."
—Linus Pauling, American chemist and winner of the Nobel Peace Prize (but not a YouTuber)

Take Action

Hopefully you've already started thinking about ideas for videos. If not, take some time to think of a few now. Use the tips in this chapter! As you come up with them, type them into your phone or write them down, because you'll want to remember them later when you actually set up your camera or your phone to shoot your video!

SCRIPTING YOUR VIDEOS AND COMING UP WITH THINGS TO SAY

Now that you have an idea for your video, where do you start? What do you say?

Scripting Your Video

Depending on how complicated your video is, it may be easiest to write down everything you want to say. For example, you're making a video about UFO conspiracy theories, and there are fifteen conspiracies you want to talk about. You could list them and write up a few sentences about each one of them before you ever start shooting your video. Then, when you shoot, you can refer

> **PRO TIP:**
> Even popular YouTubers script their videos. Maybe not every video, but definitely some of them!

to your "script" so you are sure to cover all fifteen conspiracies!

Your script doesn't have to be in any particular format. It just needs to contain all the words you're going to say, organized in normal sentences. Here's a short example.

> "Hey YouTube! You know I love conspiracy theories, and I think you guys love them too. Well, I've found FIFTEEN OF THEM and they're going to blow your minds.
>
> "Conspiracy theory number one! Some people think that UFOs are actually humans from the future. They've invented time travel, and they travel back to where we are now, and they fly around in flying saucers. So they aren't aliens at all, but future humans! That's why some quote-unquote aliens look so much like regular people!
>
> "Conspiracy theory number two! . . ."

And on and on, until you cover all fifteen theories. That's all your script needs to contain!

I like writing scripts beforehand because then I can take my time to figure out what to say, and come up with better jokes. And sometimes I think of more details about the topic while I'm writing, and it makes my video better!

Talking Points

But sometimes you know a topic well enough that you only need to jot down the fifteen things you want to mention in your video. In this case, you don't need to write exactly what you're going to say for each one. It's faster and easier just to write talking points.

Here's what our UFO conspiracy theories topic would look like as talking points:

- ❏ 1. I love conspiracy theories
- ❏ 2. Fifteen theories
    - o   UFOs are humans from the future
    - o   Aliens control the government right now
    - o   Men in Black keep people quiet
    - o   Men in Black are aliens
    - o   1973, Holloman Air Force Base
- ❏ . . . and so on.

When you're making your video, you can just glance at each talking point to remember what to talk about. That way, you don't have to memorize all fifteen of them.

Just Talking

Or you might be lucky; you might just be a natural speaker or storyteller with a great memory. In that case, all you need to do is decide what you want to talk about, or think about, the topic you're covering in the video, and you can just turn on the camera and start talking!

That's not the case for most of us; we need a script or a list of talking points. But if you're a natural talker, then there's no need to write out talking points or a script.

Regardless of whether you use a script or talking points, or if you just wing it, your video is going to need three things, and these three things are the same in every video. The three things are: a beginning, a middle, and an end.

Beginning, Middle, and End

Believe it or not, the majority of videos follow the same old formula: "Tell 'em what you're gonna tell 'em. Then, tell 'em. Then, tell 'em what you told 'em." It sounds ridiculous, but it works, and you'll probably see it in videos all the time now that you know about it. Here's an example:

"Hi, I'm Grace Helbig, and for fun, I thought we would cook a pizza." Then Grace makes a pizza, and makes jokes while she's doing it. At the end she says, "So that's how NOT to cook a pizza, especially if you want to impress any of your friends. This was a disaster. I don't know."

She followed the old formula. First, she told you what she was going to tell you: how to make a pizza. Then, she told you / showed you, by

Grace Helbig (one of my favorite YouTubers!) with a slice of the pizza she tried to make.

making a pizza and making jokes. And finally, she told you what she told you: we tried to make a pizza, but it 100% failed.

More Brainstorming Tips

If you know what you want to talk about, but you can't think of things to say, it's all right. Just spend some time thinking about the topic, and see what comes into your mind. Put them on your phone, type them in your computer, or write them down. Don't limit yourself. Just note everything you think of.

And don't rush it. If you want to spend a whole day with the topic in the back of your mind, that's fine. Every time a new idea comes up, add it to your list. Don't filter it, and don't tell yourself, "That's a bad idea." Just list every idea you have.

Then, when you're ready to make your video, look at all your ideas. Put them into some kind of order if that helps. Get rid of the ones that don't fit, or the ones that you don't want to talk about or demonstrate.

You can use that list as talking points! Or, you can read and reread that list while you're writing your script. Either way, you've captured a bunch of great thoughts about your topic, and you can use all those ideas in your video.

Take Action

Now is the time to decide on the one topic for your video. Think about what you want to say and do in your video, and then write your script or talking points (or just psych yourself up to talk and act spontaneously).

But before you start recording, let's talk about your smile.

HOW TO BE COMFORTABLE (AND LIKEABLE) ON CAMERA

Happy, Happy, Happy

On YouTube, everyone loves seeing you be happy. Lucky for you, it's fun and easy to make videos, so it's easy to look happy when you're shooting!

A lot of YouTubers who talk to the camera get themselves pumped up before they shoot each shot. Some of us jump around the room and laugh. Some of us take a bunch of deep breaths and get excited.

And then we jump in front of the camera and talk. (Wearing a big smile!)

We talk like we're talking to a friend. In fact, that's a great trick that you can use.

PRO TIP:
Before you shoot a video, it helps to jump around and get yourself hyped up!

Talk to Your Friend

Picture a friend who laughs at all your jokes. Someone who's really supportive of you. Some-one you like a lot.

Then, when you're making your video, tell yourself that you're only making the video for that friend! That friend is

Me and Big Man Tyrone, smiling in a video we made together.

the only one who is ever going to see this. All you have to do is talk to them. And maybe make them laugh, or get them pumped about whatever you're talking about.

You've known this person for a long time, right? Talk to them like that! Your videos will come out great!

SETTING UP YOUR PHONE, TABLET, OR VIDEO CAMERA

Shooting with a Phone or Tablet

(If you own a video camera, you can skip this part.)

Your cell phone or tablet can probably shoot videos that are just as high-quality as a video camera. But there are two things to keep in mind.

1. Make sure your phone or tablet is sideways, not vertical. The YouTube screen is horizontal.

Don't hold your phone upright like this.

Hold your phone sideways, like this!

2. Phones and tablets usually have two cameras: front-facing and rear-facing. One of the cameras may take lower quality video than the other camera, especially if your phone/tablet is older.

A phone's front-facing camera may be a little lower quality than the rear-facing camera.

A phone's rear-facing camera usually gives the best video quality.

To check whether one camera is better than the other, make a ten-second video with one of the cameras, then make a ten-second video with the other camera. Then compare the quality of the two of them. If they're basically the same, then you can use either camera. If one of the videos is a lot better

than the other, you should make your YouTube videos with the better camera (unless that's too hard to do for some reason).

Tripod Not Required

I'll bet you don't own a tripod. That's okay! Tripods do make it easy to set up your camera and aim it, but there are other ways to set up your camera and aim it.

You can place your phone or camera on a shelf.

You can put your camera

You can put your phone on a bookshelf. (This one is leaning against a coffee mug.)

on a windowsill, too. Be sure to read the section on good lighting; it will give you tips on how to angle your camera. (Hint: Turn it a bit to the left or the right. Then when you're facing the camera, you'll have more light on one side of your face, which is what you want.)

You can also try this trick: Flip one chair over and put it on top of another chair. Then, on top of the legs, put a board, cutting board, or baking sheet. Finally, set your camera on top of that. (If you need to ask a parent for permission

A windowsill is a fine place to set your phone, but make sure it's the same height as your eyes. You may need to sit down so you're not looking down at the camera (which looks weird).

This is the wacky "stacked-chair" configuration, with a baking sheet on top.

first, DO THAT so you don't get in trouble. Show them this picture so they can see what you're going to do! It will sound crazy otherwise.)

The phone on top of the baking sheet is held up with a couple of coffee mugs, but you can use anything else that's convenient and won't slide away while you're shooting.

I held the phone myself to make a selfie-style video.

You can also just have a friend or sibling hold your camera! (Make sure they read the section about how to "frame" a shot first.)

Or, you can just hold the camera in your own hand. That's pretty easy! And it builds up the muscles in your arm. ;-)

PRO TIP:
If you can see yourself on a screen while you are shooting your video, that's ideal. Then you can see yourself, and make sure you don't wander off screen where no one can see you.

FRAMING, LIGHTING, AND SET DRESSING

T

his may sound scary or intimidating. Trust me, it's not. You can learn how to do all these things and make your videos look great!

Framing

When the camera is pointed at you, you should be in the middle of the frame. Right?

Wrong.

If a person's eyes are right in the middle of the frame, it looks weird and unbalanced.

My eyes are in the vertical center, meaning the distance from my eyes to the top of the frame is the same as the distance from my eyes to the bottom of the frame. It looks unbalanced.

Viewers expect to see YouTubers' eyes towards the top of the frame.

Now my eyes are towards the top of the frame. That looks so much better!

A lot of the time, the top of the YouTuber's head will even be cut off!

My tall hair is partially cut out of this shot. Other YouTubers crop out even more of their hair (and forehead) sometimes, depending on how close the camera is to them.

It's fine to be centered horizontally.

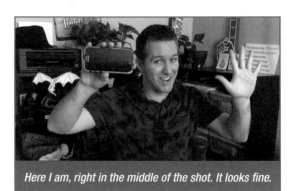
Here I am, right in the middle of the shot. It looks fine.

But a lot of the time, popular YouTubers will be more to the left, or more to the right. And they'll "teleport around" in the frame while they're talking. (We'll talk about this more in the chapter on shooting your videos.)

To make your shots particularly well balanced, you can also use an old photography technique called

YOUTUBE TALK
The "frame" is the outer border of your video or what you can see through your camera. It's the rectangle at the edge of what you see. You can see things that are "in the frame," and you can't see everything that's "outside the frame".

"the rule of thirds." The idea is that if you look at a photograph or a video, and you imagine it divided into thirds vertically and horizontally (like a tic-tac-toe board or a # hashtag), you naturally want to look at the points where the lines cross.

And that's where your face should be! More specifically, your eyes should be there, because people look at your eyes.

This is a well-framed shot.

But YouTube videos are meant to be fun and active, so don't use the rule of thirds all the time. If someone is on camera just talking and staying in the same place—even if the shot is composed perfectly— you'll probably find another video to watch. Just keep it in the back of your mind to use when you want.

If you draw a tic-tac-toe board on top of the image, you'll see that my eyes are right where two of the lines cross. They're one-third of the way down from the top, and one-third of the way from the right of the frame.

Lighting and the "Hug" Trick

The most popular YouTubers have fancy, expensive lighting setups.

Fortunately, you don't need that. There's a really simple and cheap way to light your videos. It works like this: When you're facing your camera, open your arms like you're going to give it a hug. Then freeze. Look at where your left hand is pointing, or where your right hand is pointing. That's where your light should be, either to the left or the right.

PRO TIP:

If you're shooting by a window but the daylight comes straight in, it's going to make harsh shadows that won't look good. Hang a white bedsheet over the window to diffuse the light. That will still let most of the light through, but it will look soft and good!

If you're shooting in a room with windows and it's daytime, stand with your back to the window and open your arms to give your room a hug. Look at where your left arm or your right arm is pointing; that's where you should stand for the video, and the camera should be where you are standing and hugging your room. Just turn your camera to face you. (If your arms point somewhere awkward, just take a step to your left or your right and see if it's any better. Make sure to keep your back to the window.)

A Few Things About Natural Light

Try not to have sunlight directly on you. It's too bright, and it usually makes harsh shadows that don't look so good.

Also, don't shoot at sunset unless you're making a really short video. I watched a video where the YouTuber started shooting at sunset. At the start of the video, everything looked great. At the end of the video, it was night and you couldn't see anything. (The YouTuber was still talking, though. It was pretty funny!)

Shooting outside during the day guarantees plenty of light. But it's best to stand in the shade, believe it or not! When you stand in the sun, your nose casts a dark shadow, and so does your chin, and it often doesn't look good in a video. It looks better if you're in shade—under

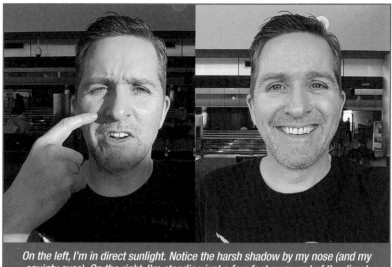

On the left, I'm in direct sunlight. Notice the harsh shadow by my nose (and my squinty eyes). On the right, I'm standing just a few feet away, out of the direct sunlight. There are no harsh shadows, and I can open my eyes.

a tree, next to a building, or blocking the sun with whatever is handy. If you have to be in direct sunlight, try to be near the white wall of a house or building, or standing on snow or sand or something white. All that white will reflect the sunshine and sort of "fill in" all those shadows.

Lamps and Ceiling Lights

If you want to shoot at night, and you're indoors, you'll need to use lamps and ceiling lights. The ceiling lights are probably in the center of the room, so you'll need to stand close to a wall, and your camera may need to be near the wall too. Don't put your camera directly under the ceiling light; you need to use the hug trick here too!

PRO TIP:
Walls reflect color, too. If you shoot in a room with red walls, everything's going to look pink! If you can shoot video in a room with mostly white or gray walls, that's probably best.

The same goes for lamps. Position them to the left or right of the camera with the hug trick. And make sure they are above your head. If they're at the same height as your head, it just looks weird. If they're

A portable work light (with a hood) clamped to a bookcase.

below you, well, that makes it look like you're in a horror film.

Make sure there are a lot of lights. The more lights, the better. If you make a video with less light, your camera has to work harder and your video will probably not have very much color in it. (Strange, but true!)

YOUTUBE TALK
The "set dressing" is decoration. It's all the stuff you "dress" your set with: pictures, action figures, flowers in a vase, book shelves, etc.

If you have a little money, and you want some more light, you can buy a portable work light. It can clamp onto a bookcase shelf, the vertical pole ("stand") of a floor lamp you're already using, or even a broomstick that you lean against the wall.

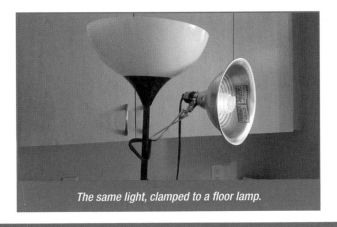

The same light, clamped to a floor lamp.

Regular light bulbs (incandescent, CFL or LED) usually make everything in a video look yellow. It's worth it to buy light bulbs that are "daylight" colored. If you've never bought lights before, you might be surprised to know that they come in slightly different colors of white. "Daylight" is one of the options. "Daylight" lights will look weird when you turn them on at night, but your phone or video camera will really like them, I promise you. Your videos will come out with better colors (and won't look yellow).

YOUTUBE TALK

Your "set" is everything that appears behind you and around you on camera. To be more accurate, it's the whole location where you're shooting your video. It's where the phrase "quiet on the set!" comes from.

Set Dressing

So you've set up your camera, you know where to position yourself in the frame, and your lighting is perfect. Now, look behind you.

This is how my set looks in videos.

What's in the background makes a difference. You want the background to be interesting, but not distracting.

Some YouTubers shoot in front of a brick fireplace, or a bookcase with books and a plant in it, or a wall on which they've taped pictures

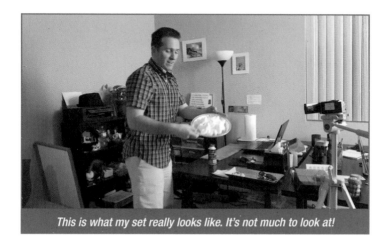

This is what my set really looks like. It's not much to look at!

and posters. Those are all good backgrounds. They give the viewer something to look at, but it won't distract them from looking at you.

But you don't want to let your little brother or sister play around in the background, because your viewers on YouTube will get distracted.

This shot is looking straight at this desk. It's fine, but it's not great.

The same goes for pets; everyone watching your video on YouTube will be looking at your pets instead of at you! (It's okay to have your pet in your video. Just hold them or play with them while you're recording.)

You can make your background more interesting by the way you set up the camera, too. Instead of pointing your camera right at whatever

This is the same desk, but I put the camera off to the left and turned back to the right. It looks a lot more interesting!

you're standing in front of, move your camera to the left a few feet and turn it back to the right.

Or shoot in a corner, like I do.

Turning the camera or shooting in a corner just looks better.

And whatever you do, don't shoot in front of a blank wall. It's too boring. (Some big YouTubers can make this work, but only if their lighting is really fancy.)

I typically shoot my videos in the corner where my desk is. The camera isn't pointed straight at either wall. It's at an angle to both of them!

Making a YouTube Studio in Your Bedroom

If you always shoot videos in your bedroom, like a lot of YouTubers do, you can turn it into a video studio pretty easily.

First, figure out where the light will be coming from (your window, if you're shooting during the day, or lamps if you're shooting at night), and where you have room to put the camera. Then, point the camera at one corner. That's where you'll shoot most of your videos.

PRO TIP: Visual contrast looks good in videos. If you're in front of a light background, wear something dark. If you're in front of a dark background, wear something light. (If your background has light and dark, you can wear whatever you want!)

"Dress" that corner. Hang pictures. Hang posters. Put a bookcase or a shelf there with a plant on it. Make sure some of them are only half visible in the frame. For example, you can tape up a poster on the right side of where you will stand so that viewers can only see the left half of it. The right half will be out of the frame. (I don't know why this looks better, but it does!)

And that's it. You have a studio in your bedroom!

You can take the camera down when you're not shooting, and if you use lamps for lighting, you can move those too. But every time you shoot, you can put the camera (and lamps) back where you've already figured out they belong.

Also, change the background "set dressing" every month or two to keep it interesting. Move things around. Put up new pictures and posters. If a fan sends you something, put that up too.

Yes, you're going to have fans. Because you're going to start shooting videos now.

SHOOTING
YOUR VIDEOS

Prepare

So, you have your script or talking points, or at least you know what you're going to talk about.

Your camera and lights are set up. You know where to appear in the frame, and what the background should look like.

You know how to be comfortable on camera, how to look excited, and how to be yourself.

Now it's time to shoot!

Quiet on the Set!

Try to limit the background noise. Turn off anything that's making noise. If you're in your house, and there are other people there too, either close a door or ask them to be quiet for fifteen minutes while you shoot.

If there's some noise, don't worry. Your video doesn't have to be perfect. Later on you can cover it up with music when you're editing. (We'll talk about that in another chapter!) Plus, noises in the background might give you opportunities for comedy. If the dog starts barking, you could say, "Yes, Muffy, is there something you wanted to say?" or "I'll take you for a walk when I'm done, I promise!"

I just tape my notes to my camera. (Or I have them on my laptop screen next to me.)

Your Script / Talking Points

If you have a script or talking points, put them somewhere out of frame but easily visible to you.

When you're shooting, read one line to yourself, look into the camera with a smile (or whatever emotion seems right for that sentence) and say the words enthusiastically. Trust me, a lot of big YouTubers do it this way!

You Can Say That Again!

If you're using a script or talking points, and something you say sounds weird, just say it again! You can say the exact same thing as many times as you want to! You can even try it once casually, and then once excitedly, and then another time with a big smile. When you're done shooting, you'll edit your video (unless you do it all perfectly the first time, which 99% of people can't).

> **PRO TIP:**
> Popular YouTubers all make mistakes when they make their videos. They just cut them out when they're editing.

Later on you can just cut out all the parts where you mess up!

That's how I do it in every one of my videos. Here's an example of me trying to say a really simple line.

Me: "And then you click on this button."

Wait, I messed up.

Me: "And then you click or tap on this button."

Wait, I wasn't smiling and relaxed. Take a deep breath . . . let it go . . . Ahhhh. Now smile like you're talking to your friend!

Me: "And then, you click or tap on THIS button!"

There, that was perfect!

Being Funny

If you want your video to be funny, make as many jokes as you can think of, whenever you think of them. Do stupid things! Run around! Be ridiculous! You don't have to include ANY of that in the final video. But when you're editing you may find that a lot of it is really fun and funny! (Everything else, you can just cut out.)

It goes without saying that viewers love YouTubers with big personalities! So the more enthusiastic and excited you get, the better! As a lot of popular YouTubers say, "I'm pretty much myself on camera, but I'm an exaggerated version of myself." So go wild!

Where to Look

While you're being hyper and fun, make sure to look into the camera most of the time. If you set up your camera so that you can see yourself on its screen, you'll be tempted to look at yourself. But don't do that! It just looks weird. You need to look at the camera lens so your viewers feel like you're looking at them. (Next time you're watching YouTube, notice that YouTubers look straight into the camera lens, like they're looking at you!)

I was looking at myself here, instead of looking at my phone's camera. It looks weird because I'm not "making eye contact" with you.

This rule of thumb is for when you're saying something or acting something out for the video. But when you're reading your script or looking at your talking points, obviously you can look at your notes. You'll edit that out later, too.

I'm looking straight at the camera here. I'm "making eye contact" with you!

Moving Around

Another thing that popular YouTubers do is teleport.

They say something, then there's a camera cut and suddenly they're in another spot. They say something else, and they teleport to the other side of the screen to say the next thing.

Everyone does that and it's easy to accomplish. Just say whatever you're saying, and then move left or right or forward or backward (or up

YOUTUBE TALK

I might be the only one who calls it "teleporting," but almost all the big YouTubers "teleport" around the screen. They are in one position, then they cut to another shot and they're some-where else in the frame.

John Green (of vlog brothers), in the first shot of his video. He's right in the middle of the frame.

or down)! When you edit the video, you will cut out the part where you move, and just keep the part where you're talking.

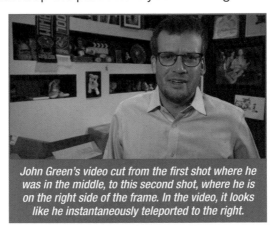

John Green's video cut from the first shot where he was in the middle, to this second shot, where he is on the right side of the frame. In the video, it looks like he instantaneously teleported to the right.

In the third shot of John Green's video, he teleported to the left of the frame.

When you're doing this, move to a new position, stop there for a moment, and look at the camera. THEN say your next sentence. Pause for a second before you move to a new spot. The reason you pause is for editing; you don't want to be moving to your next spot while you're talking. So say something, pause, then move, then pause again, say something else, pause, move, pause, say the next thing. Don't move and talk at the same time!

Props

If you feel like holding something, like a game controller or an action figure or a loaf of bread, do it! That will make your video more interesting to watch. It's especially good if it helps your video.

Me, acting out a story with dolls.

Me, creating a sci-fi / fantasy world with some props.

For example, if you're making a video about unicorns, and you have a stuffed unicorn, use it! Pretend you're having a conversation with it! Let your action figure ride it around.

Me, with a big foam finger.

And as with everything else that you shoot, if you don't like it, you can edit it out.

EDITING YOUR VIDEOS

When you're done shooting, it's time to pick what you love in your video and throw the rest away.

A Simple Editing App or Program Will Do

Don't think that you need super-fancy, expensive editing software. Really, your app or program only needs to be able to do five things:

1. Import multiple video clips (that means just bringing video into the program)

2. Import still pictures (that means bringing pictures in; we'll use pictures later on, for intros and outros)

3. Cut video clips

4. Add music on a separate track and control how loud or quiet it is

5. Save your edited video (which is usually called "exporting" the video)

If your app or program doesn't do all five things, you can't really call it a video editor!

But now that you know what features it needs, which editing app should you use?

Video Editor Apps

I've used iMovie and Adobe Premiere for editing videos. Both are just fine! Premiere has some features that iMovie doesn't, and I use them

> **PRO TIP:**
> Don't include fancy transitions in your videos. Don't make the image flip over, or fade out / fade in, or "dissolve" from one shot to another. Popular YouTubers just do a "hard cut" from one shot to the next. They just cut one shot, and start another one. That makes it look like they're teleporting around—disappearing from one place and popping up in another place.

Final Cut Pro

sometimes, but Premiere costs more. I only switched from iMovie to Premiere because I switched from a Mac to a PC, and iMovie doesn't work on a PC.

There are a lot of other video-editing apps you can look at as well. You don't need to take much time reviewing them. If they can do the

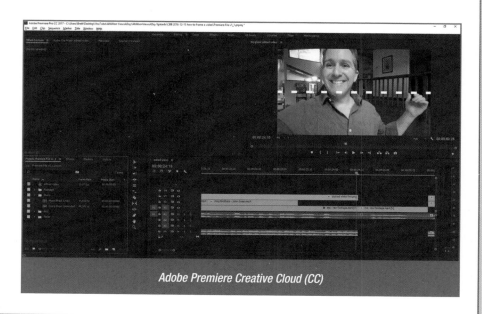

Adobe Premiere Creative Cloud (CC)

five things we talked about a second ago, just pick the one that fits in your budget. Google "video editing apps" and you'll find dozens of options.

I guarantee there are plenty of tutorials online showing you how to do any of the five things you need to do (import video, import pics, cut, add music, and export) in the app you choose.

Just remember that the program you use doesn't make your video great. You do! And it's a lot easier than you might think!

Keep Your Favorite Parts

Import your video into the editing app. Then start watching it. You'll probably notice sections where you make a mistake, but you can cut those out. Just "cut" the video before the mistake, and "cut" the video after the mistake, then delete the mistake. Depending on your video editing app, it might get rid of the "space" that you created when you deleted that part of the video. Some apps do it for you, but some let you decide if you want to leave the silent black footage or not.

You'll probably see yourself saying the same thing five times, so just cut four of them and keep the best one. Use the same steps: cut the video before, cut the video after, and delete.

Also cut out all the parts where you move from one position to another (if you aren't talking!).

The goal with editing is to create a video that has:

❑ a beginning: "Hi! I'm going to talk about [my topic]!"

❑ a middle: "Here is an example of [my topic]. Here are my thoughts on [my topic]. Oh, and here's a joke about [my topic]!"

❑ an end: "So that's everything I want to tell you about [my topic]! Be sure to subscribe, and I'll see you in the next video!"

So keep enough of your video to cover these three parts!

(Of course, you can ignore this whole editing section if you just turn on the camera, talk, and don't make a mistake. If you can do that, I'm really, really impressed with you!)

Edit for Sound

But how closely should you cut a video? Do you leave one or two seconds at the beginning of each clip and at the end of each clip?

Most popular YouTubers edit for sound. That is, they don't leave a lot of silent pauses. Cut the video when you first start saying the first

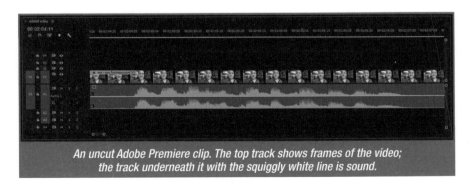

An uncut Adobe Premiere clip. The top track shows frames of the video; the track underneath it with the squiggly white line is sound.

word of your sentence. Then cut the video after the last sound of the last word of your sentence. Keep that clip.

YOUTUBE TALK
A "clip" is just a short section of a video. When you cut your video before it, and cut your video after it, the piece in the middle is a "clip," also known as a "video clip."

If you run together a bunch of clips that are edited for sound, your whole video will be full of important stuff. It will make you sound clever and quick-witted and enthusiastic.

Most video editing apps show a track for video, and another track for audio (sound). The louder the sound, the higher the squiggly line on the audio track.

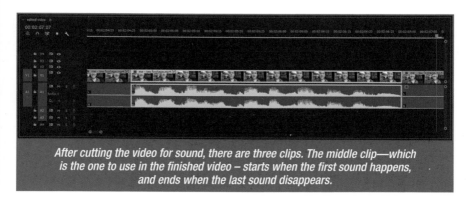

After cutting the video for sound, there are three clips. The middle clip—which is the one to use in the finished video – starts when the first sound happens, and ends when the last sound disappears.

You just find where the line on the audio track switches from flat to squiggly, or squiggly to flat, and cut there.

In the Adobe Premiere images, you probably noticed that there are two squiggly lines on the audio track, but they look the same. One is for the sound coming out of the left speaker, and one is for the sound coming out of the right speaker. They look the same because when I recorded the video, both sides were as loud as each other. If one side was louder, the squiggly line for that side would be taller.

Editing Takes a Long Time

Even if you make a short video, you're probably going to be editing for a long time. I usually shoot a video in about 10 minutes, then I spend one to two hours editing it, cutting out all the parts where I messed up or changed position or whatever.

It takes everyone a long time to edit. That includes Shane Dawson and Grace Helbig and Philip DeFranco and PewDiePie. Some famous YouTubers even hire other people to edit their videos for them! (Lucky!)

Titles (Optional)

Your editing app might have the option to add "titles" (text) over the top of your videos. This is useful for step-by-step videos. Each title can describe a step onscreen: "Step 1: Crack the eggs into the bowl." "Step 2: Add vanilla extract and milk." "Step 3: Whisk until frothy."

A subtitle from one of my videos.

You can use titles just to display the video title at the start of your video. For example, "Building an Awesome Snowman."

You can use them if someone says something in the background, and it's hard to hear but you want to include it anyway. You should probably show that as a subtitle, which just means a text title at the bottom of the screen, usually with double quotes around it, "like this".

A Few Other Advanced Features

Your editing app probably has a bunch of other features that you'll never use. But there are a few you might find that could come in handy.

❑ "Picture in picture". This is used in most gaming videos. The player is in a small box

PRO TIP:
If you use white balance, contrast, and/or saturation in your editing app, apply them to your video before you start cutting it up. In some programs, if you cut your video into twenty different clips, you would need to apply white balance, contrast, and/or saturation to each of those twenty clips separately!

in the corner, and the gameplay takes up the rest of the screen.

❑ "Zoom" or "scale". If you increase the zoom or the scale, it will look as though you're closer to whatever is in the video. The outside edges of the video will disappear off the edge of the viewable window. Once you're "zoomed in" a little bit, you can pan around the image.

❑ "Pan". This is not about frying pans. It's about moving around the image. If there are two things on screen, and you want the camera to move from one to another, first zoom in on one of them by changing the "zoom" or "scale," then "pan" to the other in your editing software.

❑ "White balance" or "color temperature". If your editing app has this feature, it's pretty handy. Typically, you select this option and then click on a part of the image that is white or gray. It tells the program how to adjust the color of the whole video so it looks more normal. For instance, if your video is too blue, or too yellow, using the "white balance" will eliminate the excess blue or yellow.

PRO TIP:
Using a format of "h.264" produces high-quality video, and the editing app I use allows me to pick that. Also, I export my videos to be the same size as the video I shoot, which is "Full HD" (1920 pixels by 1080 pixels, also called 1080p). But if you don't have one or both of those options on your video, just choose the highest-quality export it lets you choose.

❑ "Contrast". When you increase contrast, the dark areas get darker and the bright areas get brighter. I sometimes increase the contrast just a tiny bit on my videos to make them look more punchy.

❑ "Saturation". This is like contrast, but for colors; higher saturation means redder reds, bluer blues, and greener greens. 0% saturation means everything is shades of gray.

Each app may name these differently, so for example you could Google "set white balance in [your video editor app]".

Export vs. Save

So you're all done editing your video! Now it's time to save it.

But it's probably not called save! "Save" will save the project that you've edited, with all the cuts and everything else you did, but you can't upload that to YouTube. You will probably still need to find an option that says "Export," or "Export Media," or "Export Video".

That will create a video file that YouTube can accept. YouTube currently takes a lot of different formats: MOV, MP4 (MPEG4), AVI, WMV, FLV, 3GP, MPEGPS, and WebM.

UPLOADING
TO YOUTUBE

Congratulations! You made a great video! Now you'll upload it to your YouTube channel!

When you upload, YouTube is going to ask you about your video. The better you describe your video, the more views you will get! The information YouTube collects about your video is called "metadata" (pronounced "MET-uh DAY-tuh"). That is what YouTube uses to recommend your video to viewers, through search and through recommended videos. Since your video's metadata is so important, we'll discuss that first. When we're done with the metadata, we'll go through the steps for uploading your video to YouTube.

Title, Description, and Tags (Metadata)

The most important metadata to YouTube is your video's title, description, and tags. This is the only way YouTube knows what your video is about! (No, YouTube can't "watch" your video and know what's in it.) When a random person in the world goes to YouTube

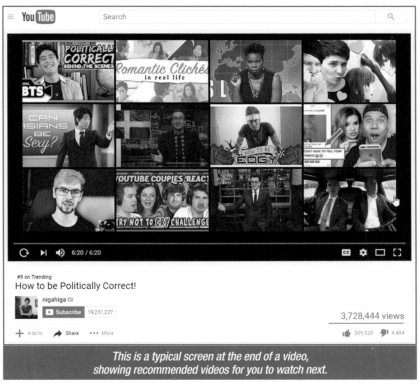

This is a typical screen at the end of a video, showing recommended videos for you to watch next.

and types something in the search box, YouTube looks for videos that have those same words in the title, in the description, and in the tags. If your video's metadata matches the search terms, then YouTube will show it higher in the search results.

> **YOUTUBE TALK**
> "Search terms" are what someone types into the search box on YouTube. For example, "funny puppy video" may be a search term.

YouTube also uses your video's metadata to recommend it at the end of other videos. You know how YouTube chooses all of those recommended videos? It picks them based on your video's metadata. If the metadata for the video that just finished is similar to yours, then YouTube will often recommend your video as the next one to watch. And that means more views for you!

The best way to come up with a title, description, and tags for your video is to think about what random people in the world might type in when they're looking for a video like yours. For example, if your video is about washing your dog, that random person might type in any of these:

- ❑ how to wash a dog
- ❑ how to wash your dog
- ❑ washing a dog
- ❑ give a dog a bath
- ❑ bathing your dog
- ❑ bathe my dog
- ❑ wash dog
- ❑ dog bath
- ❑ doggie bath
- ❑ cute dog
- ❑ cute dog video

(There are probably a hundred other things you can think of. These are just a few ideas.)

Create that list first, then pick one or two of the phrases for your title. Here are a few you could use:

- ❑ How to Wash Your Dog
- ❑ How to Wash Your Dog (Cute Dog!!)
- ❑ DOG BATH – How to wash your dog

For your video description, write some normal sentences describing your video, and be sure to include a few of those search terms in them. Here's an example:

"I gave my cute dog a doggie bath! It's usually hard washing a dog, but my dog Hattie really seems to like it. Enjoy this cute dog video!"

That's normal English, but it includes all of these phrases that people might type in: "cute dog," "doggie bath," "washing a dog," "cute dog" (again), and "dog video". And every sentence includes the word "dog" at least once, which really tells YouTube that this video is about dogs!

It may seem like a good idea just to list all the search phrases in your video's description, but don't do that! It's against YouTube rules, and YouTube can remove your video if you do that! In your description, those phrases can only be included in normal sentences.

But in your tags, you are supposed to list all those words and phrases you came up with. So pick 10 to 15 of them and put those in the "Tags" fields. Make sure to separate your tags. On a laptop, you can do that by putting commas between phrases, or by pressing Enter between phrases. The YouTube app works differently. We'll discuss that later.

Some YouTube tags.

If you make a mistake when you're entering tags, don't worry. You can always go back and edit your video's metadata after it's uploaded.

Public, Unlisted, and Private (More Metadata)

The "privacy" setting of your video determines who can see it. This is part of your video's metadata too.

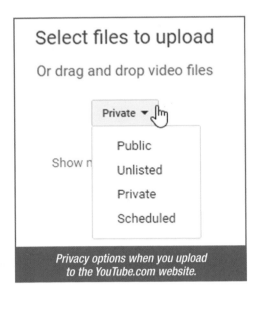

Privacy options when you upload to the YouTube.com website.

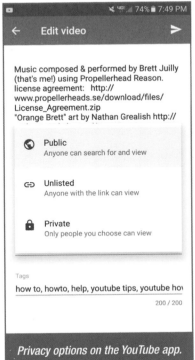

Privacy options on the YouTube app.

- ❏ "Public" means everybody on YouTube can see it.

- ❏ "Unlisted" means anyone who has the web address for your video can view it. If you want people to see your video on a website or in a vlog, but not directly on YouTube, you can use this option. Then you embed the web link in your site or vlog. You can also send the link to friends.

- ❏ "Private" means that nobody can see the video, unless you invite them. For example, if you invite User1234, then User1234 can see it (if they're signed into YouTube). But no one else can, except for you.

- ❏ "Scheduled" isn't always available, it isn't available in some countries, and it isn't available to some users. But if you see this option, it means you can set a time that everyone will get to see your video. Say you set the schedule for tomorrow at noon. Before then, the video will be Private. At noon tomorrow, your video will automatically switch to Public, meaning everybody on YouTube can see it.

You'll learn the best way to use these when we talk about uploading your video.

Thumbnail (Even More Metadata)

The small picture that represents a video is called its thumbnail (or its thumbnail image or thumbnail picture). It's another piece of metadata for your videos.

Your title, description, and tags allow people to find your video. Your thumbnail picture makes people tap or click on your video to watch it.

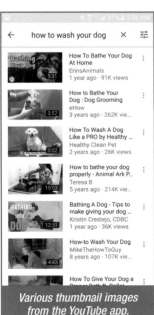

Various thumbnail images from the YouTube app.

You can make a thumbnail image using Adobe Photoshop or another image editing program. "GIMP" is a popular free program you can use to make thumbnails.

The GIMP website (gimp.org).

Follow these tips to make a thumbnail image that will stand out and get clicked:

❑ Show someone's face (or your dog's face) in your thumbnail. Make sure they're looking at the camera, they take up a lot of space in the image, and they have a big expression! (That might be smiling, furious, startled, or whatever works for your video.)

❑ Keep your thumbnail simple. Sometimes the thumbnail is shown really, really small, and people will only glance at it for half a second!

❑ Use bright colors (unless it is very serious and dark grays make sense).

❑ Use contrast. Include some bright parts and some dark parts.

❑ If you want to show text, use short words and limit yourself to three or four words, maximum. Make them

VLOG - Fun indoor & repas chez QUICK - Aire de jeux intérieure

Swan The Voice - Néo & Swan 3M views • 9 months ago

Swan s'amuse comme un fou dans l'aire de jeux de Quick, d'abord avec maman, puis après quelques frites et nuggets, avec Néo ...

11:49

I did a lot of fun things in this vlog.

Rachel Vlogs ✓ 187K views • 11 months ago

I ran a bunch of errands but had **fun** doing it. Nothing super exciting happened, so I couldn't come up with a title. Next video: ...

7:50

CIHAN PRANKT MILEY !! Kira erschrocken? Vlog #73 Our life FAMILY FUN

Family Fun ✓ 53K views • 15 hours ago

Cihan prankt seine Schwester Miley aus Langeweile ;-) Viel Spaß beim schauen und liken! Kanal kostenlos hier abonnieren ...

13:36   New

OP NAAR MIAMI! - Miami vlog #1 met Teske - FUN

fun ✓ 136K views • 1 year ago

Teske en ik gaan een weekje **naar Miami** en we nemen jullie mee! Vergeet niet te abonneren: http://bit.ly/AbonneerOpFUN ...

10:06

99Cent SLIME FLOAM & PUTTY VLOG & HAUL! ~ DOLLAR STORE | Sedona Fun Kids TV

Sedona Fun Kids TV 42K views • 1 week ago

Hi guys we found lots of cheap 99Cent Slime Floam & Putty in the Dollar Store! (99Cent Only Store)! My BFF Paige came slime ...

13:28

Family Vlog - Fun Day in Santa Cruz

Ballinger Family ✓ 140K views • 1 year ago

Join us as we take on the Santa Cruz Board Walk!!! Subscribe to us: http://bit.ly/19AVFM6 Check out Magic Monday: ...

6:46

Saturday Sleepover Fun - Summer Vacation VLOG 2017

Millie and Chloe DIY 48K views • 2 months ago

It's the Summer school holidays here in Australia so we have regular sleepovers at each others house. We thought you'd like to ...

7:33

These thumbnail images look great, and they mostly follow the guidelines above.

BIG and easy to read. Use capital letters. Make the text a color that stands out from the background (don't put black text on a dark gray background). Outline your letters with a contrasting color if you want to.

It's sometimes simplest to use a still image from your video. Even better than that, think about what you want your thumbnail image to look like before you start shooting your video, and then pose for it while you are shooting! That way you'll get the perfect expression (happy, surprised, serious, angry, or whatever) and you can just take that frame out of your video when you're editing!

One thing that popular YouTubers do is to make all their thumbnails look kind of similar. So no matter what your video is about, make the thumbnail look a little bit like all your other thumbnails. After you have several videos uploaded to YouTube, your fans will be able to spot your videos quickly in the search results.

Popular YouTuber Shane Dawson does a great job with this. His thumbnails almost always include his own face, along with some other elements that tie into the video. His thumbnails almost always use a bright yellow background (even if the topic is serious, like scary UFO conspiracy theories). He even reuses the same picture of himself over

BLOW TORCHING STUFF!
1,720,182 views · 3 weeks ago

CELEBRITY CONSPIRACY THEORIES
3,279,562 views · 3 weeks ago

TASTING CELEBRITIES FAVORITE FOODS 2
1,998,237 views · 4 weeks ago

MY HOUSE IS HAUNTED
2,293,557 views · 1 month ago

TRYING DUMB LIFE HACKS 12
2,635,806 views · 1 month ago

HAUNTED HOTEL
2,536,609 views · 1 month ago

Shane Dawson's thumbnails all have the same "look".

and over in a lot of them! It's simple to spot his videos because the thumbnails all look similar.

Uploading

Now you know everything you need to know about metadata. It's finally time to upload the video you made!

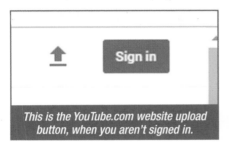

This is the YouTube.com website upload button, when you aren't signed in.

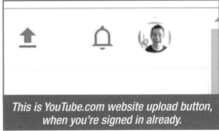

This is YouTube.com website upload button, when you're signed in already.

The upload button on the YouTube.com website and the YouTube app look different. On the website, the button looks like an arrow pointing up, with a line under it. (*Up*load . . . arrow pointing *up* . . . get it?)

The YouTube.com app upload button, which changes position on different pages of the app.

The upload button on the YouTube app looks like a red circle with a white camera in it. It used to be an arrow pointing up, with a line under it, but YouTube changed it (last time I checked).

Click or tap to start uploading. YouTube will ask you for the video file to upload, and after you select that, you'll see a screen asking for the metadata we talked so much about in the first half of this chapter!

It may seem smart to upload your video as "Public," but you should really mark it "Private". If you choose "Public," then your video starts uploading while you are still typing in metadata. You only have a few minutes to type out the title, a wonderful description, and all the right tags before your video is uploaded. If your video finishes uploading before you are finished putting in the title and description and tags, people might see your video with a half-finished title or description!

So choose "Private" when you are uploading your video. Then you can take all the time you want to create a great title, write out a great

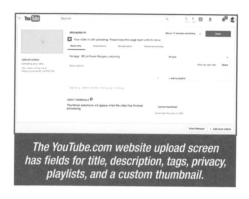

The YouTube.com website upload screen has fields for title, description, tags, privacy, playlists, and a custom thumbnail.

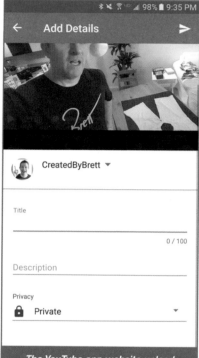

The YouTube app website upload screen only has fields for the channel to which you're uploading, and the title, description, and privacy of your video.

description, and list all your great tags. When you're done and the video is uploaded, "edit" your video and switch it from Private to Public. (More about editing your video later.)

For some reason, the YouTube website asks for more information than the YouTube app. On the YouTube website, you can enter the title, description, tags, and other stuff all at once. In the app (at the time I'm writing this), you can only enter the title and description for your video. You can't enter the tags while you're uploading.

That means that after you upload from the website, you're done, but from the app you need to go back and edit the metadata for your video.

Editing Your Metadata

From the YouTube app, tap on the "person" icon to go to your Account page. Tap on "My videos". Find the video you want to edit, and tap on the three dots to the right of it. From that menu (finally!), select "Edit".

The Edit screen in the YouTube app shows all the metadata you've entered. Switch the Privacy setting to "Public". Don't worry; no one will see the video until you tap on the white paper-airplane icon in the upper-right corner.

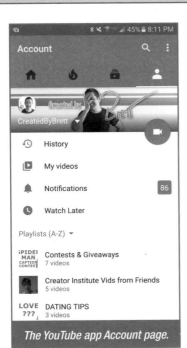

The YouTube app Account page.

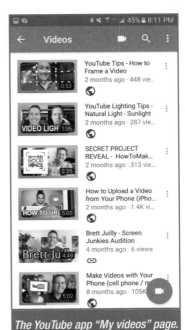

The YouTube app "My videos" page.

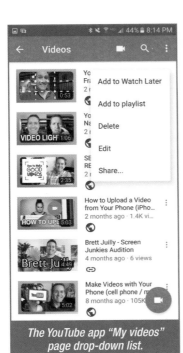

The YouTube app "My videos" page drop-down list.

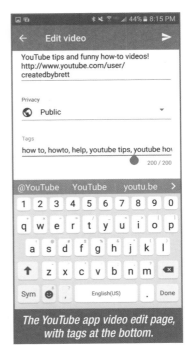

The YouTube app video edit page, with tags at the bottom.

The "Tags" field is at the bottom. Enter your tags, separated by commas. For example, if you uploaded the dog-washing video we described earlier, your tags might look like this:

how to wash a dog, how to wash your dog, washing a dog, give a dog a bath, cleaning your dog, clean my dog, wash dog, dog bath, doggie bath, cute dog, cute dog video

When you're done entering your tags, and you've changed your Privacy setting, tap on the white paper-airplane icon in the upper right corner to send your changes to YouTube.

And that's it! Your video is on YouTube!

(Note: Next time you make a video, this whole process will all go a *lot* faster for you!)

PART TWO
ADVANCED YOUTUBE

BACKGROUND MUSIC

Y ou've heard videos with background music. Most big YouTubers use music in the background. For some reason, videos with background music are just more enjoyable! There are even a few musical tricks you can use to emphasize the mood you're going for in your videos—and even make your jokes funnier! (Really!)

But first, where do you get it?

Free Music Without Copyright Issues

YouTube gives you free music!

There is a big list of songs (and sound effects) at https://youtube. com/audiolibrary. They're all free to use, and you will never get a copyright strike for using them in your videos.

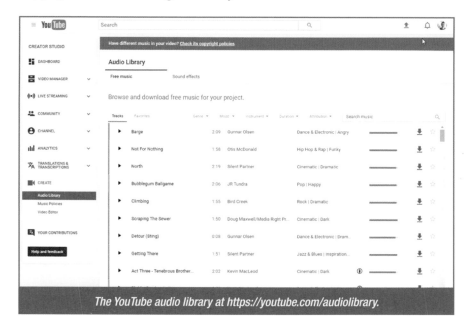

The YouTube audio library at https://youtube.com/audiolibrary.

Right now, this is easiest to use from a laptop or desktop, and it's not available on the YouTube app. (At least, I couldn't figure out how to access it!) You can listen to any song by clicking the black triangle to the left of it. Clicking on the triangle also displays more information about how you can use the music. For example, a few of the songs

Ambient Ambulance	1:20	Single Funks	Ambient	Sad	

| ▶ | Cool Intro - Stings | 0:17 | Kevin MacLeod | Rock | Funky | ⓘ — |

You're free to use this song and monetize your video, but you must include the following in your video description:

Cool Intro - Stings by Kevin MacLeod is licensed under a Creative Commons Attribution license (https://creativecomm
Source: http://incompetech.com/music/royalty-free/index.html?isrc=USUAN1100504
Artist: http://incompetech.com/

When you click on a song in the YouTube audio library, you'll see the attribution information. This tells you whether you need to mention ("attribute") it in your video description.

require that you put some text in your video description when you use the song. You just copy and paste it from the screen.

When you find songs that you like, click the downward-pointing arrow to the right of the song name. That will download the MP3 to your computer.

How to Add Music to Your Videos

Don't play the music while you're shooting your video (unless you're singing along with it!). If you play it while you're recording, and you mess up what you're saying or doing, you'll have to edit that part out of your video. You know what happens when you edit a song? It sounds jumpy and uneven and terrible. ("Terrible" is probably an exaggeration, but it sure doesn't sound good!)

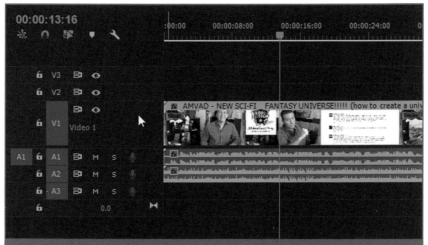

The green audio track at the bottom is background music. The blue audio track above that is from the video. The track above that with the images in it is the video (obviously).

Your video editing software can handle more than one sound (audio) track. The primary track will be your voice, talking in the video. Then you import your music into your video project, and add it on another track. Every video editing app will do this differently, so you'll need to figure out how to do that in your app.

Change the Volume

The first time you add in a song, it will probably be too loud. In fact, I can pretty much guarantee that! When your fans are watching your video, they want to hear you. If there's some quiet music in the background, they will enjoy it, but if the music makes it hard to hear what you're saying, they won't be happy campers.

So lower the volume of the music. (You'll have to find out how to do this in your particular editing app.) Lower it a lot. You probably won't get it perfect the first time, but don't worry about it. It's okay to mess up. And you'll improve with each video you make. (Everybody does!)

Your Music Folder

You're going to find some music that you like a lot, and you're going to want to use it in more than one video. Instead of downloading it every time, save it in a folder of YouTube songs.

A lot of big YouTubers have about 10 songs that they use. Each of the songs is a different mood: maybe one that's goofy clarinet, one that's tough electric guitar, one that's classical and serious, one that's excited electronica, and so on. When those big YouTubers (like D-Trix, Mamrie Hart, and Tyler Oakley) make a video, they use a song from their folder for each of the moods that they want in the video. (Part of the video is goofy, part of it's tough so it needs electric guitar, etc.)

Adding in a Mix of Music

When you're editing your videos, you might have different sections with different moods. Your videos will sound a lot more professional if you use different music in different parts.

When you're just talking, use your "fun and casual" music in the background. If one section is supposed to be sad, use the "sad" music from your music folder. For a goofy, silly part of your video, use your "goofy" music.

Also, here's an advanced trick: When you make a joke, stop the music when you say the punchline. Keep it off for a second or two after the punchline. Then start it again when you start talking again in the video. For some reason that makes your viewers *want* to laugh out loud, maybe to fill in the silence. Films and TV shows have been doing this for decades, and big YouTubers (like IISuperwomanII and Ryan Higa) use the same trick!

VIDEO INTROS
AND OUTROS

Intros Are Easy

A lot of big YouTubers have an intro they use to begin every video. When you watch one of their videos, you expect to hear that intro.

When you're a new YouTuber without a lot of fans (yet), having an intro is really helpful. Your viewers get familiar with it. They like it. They

Ryan Higa starts his videos by saying "Hey guys!" on his YouTube channel.

expect it. It makes them happy to hear it at the start of every video! And it makes them remember you.

The secret is that most intros, even from big YouTubers, are really simple. A lot of big YouTubers just have a tagline that they say!

- ❏ Ryan Higa just says, "Hey guys!" while his goofy music plays in the background.

- ❏ D-Trix starts his videos by yelling, "What's up, y'all? It's ya boy, D-Trix. We're back at it again with (whatever type of video he's doing)."

- Toby Turner, in his old Lazy Vlogs, points the camera at some random object on the street and says, "Audience?! Wha . . .? What are you doing looking at (whatever the random object is)?" And then he launches into his video.

Toby Turner giving his signature, "Audience?! Wha . . .? What are you doing looking at . . ." intro in a video about his new dog.

- IISuperwomanII starts her videos by saying, "What up, everyone? It's ya girl, superwoman!" and she touches her fingertips together to form the "S" for Superwoman.

IISuperwomanII making her trademark "S" with her fingers.

So pick something that you want to say as your tagline! Welcome people to your channel! Thank them for watching!

It doesn't have to be perfect at first. You'll make one video where you say it, then you'll make another video where you say it a little differently, and in your third video it will be a little different and a little easier to say, and then you'll start saying the same thing at the start of every video.

You might think that saying the same thing at the start of every video will get boring but it won't! (Just keep it kind of short. One or two sentences is plenty.)

Outros Are Easy Too

An outro is just like an intro, but it's at the end of the video. That's why it's called an *outro*! At the start, you get into your video; at the end, you get out of your video.

Here's what a typical outro sounds like: "Thanks for watching, guys! If you're not subscribed yet, remember to pound on that Subscribe button so you can see all the videos I upload. Leave me a comment if you wanna say hi, tickle the Like button, and I'll see you in a few days!"

So outros are generally longer than intros, and they include more calls to action.

Branded Intros

A lot of popular YouTubers, and some less well-known YouTubers, have a whole branded introduction to their videos that has music, sound effects, and visuals. You definitely don't need this; some of

YOUTUBE TALK

An "outro" is a short thing you do at the end of every video. It's like an intro, except at the end. (I don't know why they don't call them "endtros," but they don't.)

YOUTUBE TALK

A "call to action" is a request for your viewers to do something. The most common example is when a YouTuber says to his/her viewers, "Please subscribe!"

the biggest YouTubers don't have anything fancy like this! But if you want it, and you have the time and skills to make it (or your friends have the skills and the time), then go ahead and make it. Branded intros usually include either a picture on animation that shows your channel name, and they include a musical jingle (like a short theme song) or a signature sound.

Jingles

You can probably guess what a musical jingle is. It's a short song that everyone associates with your videos. It's like your theme song. It may be people singing the name of your channel, or it may just be music without words.

Most big YouTubers use a five- to six-second jingle, if they use one at all. Make sure yours is less than 10 seconds.

You can make a jingle using royalty-free music from the YouTube Audio Library. Just take a song you like, put it in your video editing app, and cut out everything but five or six seconds that you like! You might even fade out the end, if you know how to do that.

You could even play two songs at the same time in your video editing app, if they have the same beat, to make a completely new jingle no one has ever heard before! Or you could play the drums and percussion from one song with the music from another. There are a lot of creative options.

When you've got five or six seconds that you like, save (export) the video file. (Some video editing apps even let you save it as an MP3! That's better because you don't need the whole video, just the music.

Signature Sounds

It's a *lot* easier to make a signature sound than a jingle.

First off, you don't need any musical talent! A signature sound is just a noise or a few noises put together. And when people hear it, they still think of your YouTube channel and your videos.

> **YOUTUBE TALK**
>
> A "jingle" is a short bit of music, usually under 10 seconds long. Sometimes it includes singing too.

Audio Library

Free music   **Sound effects**

Browse and download free sound effects for your project.

Sounds	Favorites		Category ▼	Search sound effects			
▶	Manual Drill	0:54	Tools		▬▬	⬇	☆
▶	Alien Squawk Echo	0:47	Horror		▬	⬇	☆
▶	Bowling Alley	0:27	Sports		▬▬	⬇	☆
▶	Metal Strike on Wood	0:31	Impacts		▪	⬇	☆
▶	Slide Whistle Crazy Series	0:37	Cartoon		▬▬	⬇	☆
▶	Manure Spreader	3:23	Tools		▪	⬇	☆

Here are just a few of the sound effects on the YouTube audio library. YouTube provides them for free! (Yes, the bottom one is "manure spreader". Unfortunately, it's not funny like I hoped it would be.)

If you have a comedy channel, your signature sound could be the sound of an audience laughing while you say "Jessica, you are so-o-o funny!" (if your name is Jessica). If you have a channel about auto repair, maybe it's the sound of an impact torque wrench removing lug nuts and a throaty engine revving.

If you want some inspiration for sounds that you can use, just listen to some of the free sound effects on www.youtube.com/audiolibrary/

soundeffects. There are also a bunch more on www.soundjay.com.

If you can't get what you need from those sites, get creative! Let's say you're making a channel with your dog. Make a 30-second video of your dog barking, and use five

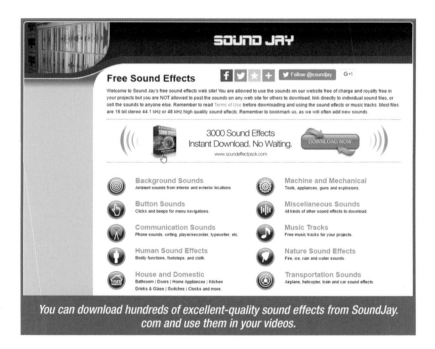

You can download hundreds of excellent-quality sound effects from SoundJay. com and use them in your videos.

seconds of that sound! If you're making a channel about basketball, go shoot video of some people playing a pickup game on a court, then use five seconds of that!

Once you've got the sounds you want to use, the editing process is just the same as creating a jingle. Put them in your video editor, cut out all the parts you don't want, and save (export) it.

Intro Screens

If you are going to use a jingle or signature sound, you should probably show something on the screen while you're playing it.

My super-fancy intro screen that my graphic designer friend made for me. (I'm not artistic enough to make something that looks this good!)

The intro screen for the Flying Kittens channel.

Arnold Telagaarta's intro screen. That looks professional!

This can be simple text on a colored background. It could be a photo. It could be a combination of text, photos and things you drew, all put together in a graphics program. (As I mentioned earlier, GIMP is a free app for editing and combining pictures. You'll be able to make an intro screen with it!)

There's a trick you can use to make sure it looks good: Find a video with an intro screen you like, and copy their layout. For example, if they have the channel name across the top with a picture in the lower half of the screen, then you would put your channel name across the top with one of your own pictures in the lower half. Change the background colors too, and you'll have a good-looking intro screen.

Intro Animation

Intro animations are a bit harder, but you can do some simple animation pretty easily. Video editing apps like Adobe Premiere, iMovie, and Final Cut let you put two or more pictures on the screen and move them

Grace Helbig's name flies across the screen at the start of her branded intro.

Grace Helbig's name floats to the center of the screen and stops there at the end of her branded intro.

around relative to each other. (We're not talking Pixar-quality animation, but it's plenty good for a quick YouTube channel intro.)

That's all YouTube superstar Grace Helbig does for her branded intros. Her name flies across the screen in one direction (while her signature sound goes "bing!"), then her name floats back down to the center of the screen (while her signature sound goes "bong").

Cheating (In a Good Way)

If this all sounds like a lot of work, you can find intros that other YouTubers have made for you to use. (Yes, some people upload videos that are just intros!) One YouTuber you might want to check out is

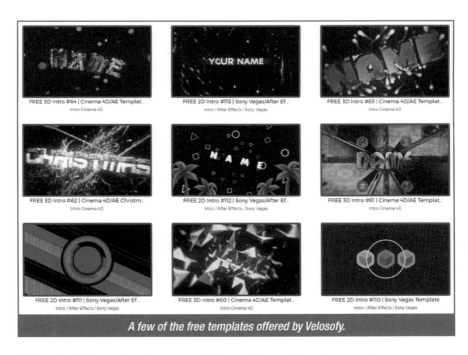

A few of the free templates offered by Velosofy.

Velosofy. He makes two- and three-dimensional computer-generated intros that you can download and customize, though I think you need some graphics software to do the editing.

Velosofy includes music with the intros he makes, but it may not all be royalty-free, so I'd recommend replacing that music with a jingle or signature sound that you create yourself.

Putting the Intro Pieces Together

So you have your jingle or your signature sound, and you have your intro screen or intro animation. The final step is to bring both clips into your video editing app, and line them up so the sound starts at about the same time as the visual element. Make sure the total video is at least three or four seconds long, but no longer than ten seconds. And then export that short little video!

Make It Easy to Repeat

Save your branded intro someplace where it will be easy to find. Every time you make a video, bring that tiny video file into your editing program. Put that intro at the start of your video.

(The alternative is recreating your video intro every time you make a new video, and that's just too much work!)

BrettFromLA Intro Screen v2.mov	1/26/2014 1:30 PM	MOV File	758 KB
CreatedByBrett intro only.mov	6/7/2014 3:40 PM	MOV File	436 KB
Happy Face.png	6/3/2016 9:53 PM	PNG File	30 KB
LATalentShow Logo.png	8/3/2014 5:40 PM	PNG File	108 KB
Laura's Happy Channel intro.m4v	5/30/2011 4:07 PM	M4V File	181 KB
outro screen.png	6/4/2014 7:07 PM	PNG File	8,135 KB
outro screen.psd	6/4/2014 7:07 PM	Adobe Photoshop...	1,144 KB

This is from my YouTube folder. I still have intro and outro videos for different YouTube channels and shows I've experimented with since 2006. ("Happy Face.png" is just a picture of a yellow happy face that I use in videos sometimes.)

Cold Openings

There's just one more element that you may want to add to the start of your video. In the last few years, a lot of famous YouTubers have started using a "cold opening". YouTube recommends these, too.

A cold opening is just a few seconds of video that viewers get

YOUTUBE TALK

A "cold opening" is a quick moment before your video really "starts," where you say what the video is about, or make a joke, or show a mistake that happened while you were shooting the video.

to see before your branded intro, or before you "officially" start your video. Cold openings sometimes have a "behind the scenes" feel. You might show a funny mistake you made while you were shooting the video. Or you might just casually tell your viewers what the video is about, or tell them what they're in for emotionally ("You guys, I

A cold opening from Shane Dawson and Gabbie Hanna (from The Gabby Show). They're both cracking up even though the rest of the video is really spooky!

got totally freaked out when I was making this video! Make sure *all the lights are on* before you keep watching!")

Immediately after your cold opening, show your branded intro, and/or say the tagline that you start your videos with.

The emotion of your cold opening can be totally different from your video intro. In your cold opening, you might be "freaked out" about something scary, and then be cheery in your video intro: "Hey subscribers! Welcome back! And if you're new to my channel, welcome for the first time! Today I'm going to be watching more YouTube ghost videos that you guys sent to me."

Branded Outros

You can use jingles, signature sounds, pictures, and animation at the end of your video as well. But viewers are also used to their favorite YouTubers talking to them directly and saying something a little different at the end of each video.

One option is to choose outro music, and make an outro picture that has a space for a small-sized video on it. The outro picture has some calls to action (like "Subscribe!" "Click the Like button!" "Share on Twitter & Facebook!"). It also has a space where you can put a video of you talking to your viewers! In most video editing apps, you can shrink the size of your video using the "scale" or "zoom" feature, and then you can "pan" it into place!

Watch another video or 5!

My outro screen from AMillionViewsADay.

Put It All Together

So now you've got a tagline for your intro and possibly a tagline for your outro. You might have a branded intro or outro. And you've decided whether you want to show a cold opening or not.

Here's the order they all go in your video:

1. Cold opening.
2. Branded intro.
3. Intro tagline.
4. Most of your video!
5. Outro tagline and calls to action ("Tickle that subscribe button!").
6. Branded outro.

(If you made a fancy outro screen that lets you show a small-sized video of yourself talking, then steps 5 and 6 happen at the same time.)

If you don't have some of those pieces, just leave them out. But the order of the remaining elements stays the same.

All these things probably weren't as complicated as you thought they would be, right? Now that you know all the pieces that go into a branded intro or outro, you know what a tagline is, and you know what a cold opening is, your videos are going to look a lot more polished. You're going to look like you're an experienced YouTuber. And you're going to get more views, shares, likes, and subscribers!

But there are even more things that you can include in the body of your videos that will make you even more popular!

PRO TIP:
Some big YouTubers even display their last video on the screen, with the sound turned down, and they tell viewers to watch it.

"CUT SCENES"

What the Heck is a Cut Scene?

In the middle of your video, you may want to demonstrate something. So you cut to a different location, do a short scene, and then cut back to you talking.

You "cut"—you show a "scene"—it's a "cut scene"!

*llSuperwomanll (Lilly Singh) is the queen of cut scenes!
Here she is playing her mom in a cut scene, in the middle of her video,
"Types of Parents".*

How to Shoot a Cut Scene

Let's say your video is about ordering food at a fast-food restaurant. You're talking about how the cashier behind the counter always wants to sell you more food. And you want to include a cut scene where you act out your typical interaction with the cashier. You'll need to plan the scene before you shoot it.

Most YouTubers will play all the parts. In other words, you will be yourself, ordering the food, and you will also be the cashier behind the counter. Since you can only play one person at a time, you will need to plan the conversation between the two characters, and then shoot each part separately. Here's a sample script:

You: "I'd like a Hamburger Deluxe."

Cashier: "Hamburger Deluxe. Do you want to mega-size that?"

You: "No, just the Hamburger Deluxe."

Cashier: "What do you want to drink?"

You: "No drink. Just the Hamburger Deluxe."

Cashier: "Do you want fries?"

You: "No, I just want the Hamburger Deluxe!"

Cashier: "You can add a Swirly Fudge Sundae for just a dollar more."

You: "I JUST WANT MY HAMBURGER DELUXE!"

Cashier: (checks behind him) "Oh . . . I'm sorry, we're out of Hamburger Deluxes."

You: (scream)

As you can see, it's a short little scene, and it's exaggerated to make it funny.

You're going to shoot all your lines as the cashier, then move the camera, and shoot all of your lines as yourself. It will be weird the first time you do this. You might even have to say all of the lines for BOTH characters just to make it sound normal! But you can edit out any lines you don't need.

Three Essentials

When you shoot a cut scene, there are three things you'll need to remember.

Cut scene of Lilly "IISuperwomanII" Singh, playing her dad. She's on the right-hand side of the frame, looking left.

1. Each character should look a little different. You can change your shirt, put on a jacket, or wear a hat or glasses or fake moustache.

2. Move the camera to a different place than your main video. It could be a different room of your house, or it could just be a different part of the room that you're shooting in.

The same cut scene of Lilly "llSuperwomanll" Singh, playing herself. She's on the left side of the frame, looking right.

3. Position yourself in the frame on the left side looking to the right, or the right side looking to the left. This is supposed to be a conversation between two people, and that's how they're always done in movies, TV, and online video.

After you shoot both parts, change back into the clothes you were wearing before, and put the camera back where it was, so you can keep shooting your "main" video (the part before you shot your cut scene).

Editing a Cut Scene

It takes a while to edit cut scenes, because you have two or more video clips that you need to blend together. But the process is pretty much the same as the rest of your video: cut out all the parts where you mess up, and keep the best version of each "line" that you say.

Once you have created all those clips of each thing that you say, just drag them around until they're in the right order. In our scene, you will alternate the clips between the cashier and yourself, since one character says something and the other character responds. It's a simple back-and-forth.

PRO TIP:

You can shoot your entire "main" video of you talking first. Then shoot your cut scene. Sometimes it's easier that way! When you're editing, you'll just put the cut scene where it belongs in the middle of the video.

One difference about editing cut scenes is that you may want to leave some silence at the start or end of some of the clips. It's supposed to sound like a normal conversation. People pause in normal conversations. Sometimes they take a moment to think about their response to what someone just said. Play around with that until you like the way it sounds. (In our scene, you would probably use less and less silence since the scene shows that you're getting more and more frustrated! People tend to answer faster when they're frustrated.)

When you're done editing your cut scene, just move all those shots into the middle of the video where they belong!

MEMORABLE THINGS YOUR FANS WILL LOVE

What the YouTube Stars Do

Did you notice that a lot of YouTube stars have "shows" that they repeat?

That they have jokes that they repeat?

That they use the same characters in different videos?

Their fans love that. Your fans will love that too. And it's pretty easy to do.

Ryan Higa has a show on his channel called "Dear Ryan".
He makes videos based on requests from viewers,
and he shows their requests at the start of the video!

Dominic "D-Trix" Sandoval, youtube.com/theDOMINICshow

D-Trix is a super-popular YouTuber who has a lot of things he repeats from video to video. He re-uses sound effects. They're hard to write about, but if you watch some of his videos, you'll notice them. There is a sound effect where he says "bonk," funny musical "stingers" he sticks in, familiar background music, etc.

He speeds up sections to show the passage of time. (When he does this, he plays a country hoedown song he got for free from Apple iLife.)

He drops silly-looking drawings on top of his video when he's editing, and makes them fly around – or he "punches" them and makes them fly off screen.

A D-Trix food challenge video, with an animated Dwayne Johnson picture added in.

He also reuses formats for shows he does. For instance, he does "food challenge" videos where he and his friends set out way too much food, then they eat it all in 10 minutes while making jokes. That's the overall idea for the show. But the format is this:

- ❑ D-Trix sits on a wide couch by himself, and introduces the show.

- ❑ As he introduces each of his friends, they "magically appear" on the couch.

- ❑ They introduce the food and it all "magically appears" in front of them.

- ❑ They eat in fast motion. Every 5 or 10 seconds, they slow down to normal speed so someone can make a joke. The music stops while they make the joke. (It's more funny when you stop the music for some reason!)

- ❑ Cut-out photos or pictures will pop up on screen every now and then for commentary.

- ❑ They take a break after five minutes of eating, and make a bunch of bad puns about the food they're eating. After almost every bad pun, he displays a red "X" over the person's face and plays a loud harsh buzzer sound. Finally, one of the jokes/puns is good enough and makes them all laugh, and he displays a green check mark over that person's face and plays a happy bell-dinging noise.

- ❑ They start eating again, and the country hoedown music starts playing again.
- ❑ They pretend that they ate all the food (even though they didn't).
- ❑ Then the music stops, D-Trix looks around at his guests, and suggests, "Tacos?" They all decide that sounds like a good idea, and stand up and walk off camera, supposedly to get tacos (even though they just ate way too much food!).

"Show" Ideas

I've created shows based on the day of the week with these themes:

- ❑ Tropical Tuesday, where I put on a tropical shirt, wore a flower lei and sunglasses, put tropical decorations around my "home studio," and played Hawaiian music in the background.
- ❑ Wednesday Trends-day, where I talked about trending videos.
- ❑ Invention Thursday, where I invented something based on viewer comments.

Here I am in a typical Fedora Friday video.

❑   Fedora Friday, where I wore a fedora and used music that sounded like a lively 1960s road-trip movie.

Grace Helbig does a "favorite products review" video once a month, and fashion review videos after an event like the Emmys or the Oscars. She also did "Fri-Diary" videos for a while, which she would upload on Fridays (of course!), where she showed video she shot earlier in the week as she drove around to places, met with friends, and did different things.

Shane Dawson regularly does videos about life hacks, food challenges, and creepy videos.

If you make a video one time, and you think it's a good "formula" for future videos, do another one! Call it a "show"! Tell your viewers, "I'm doing another video where I try to try to figure out what my cat is thinking!" (or whatever your "formula" is) and see if your fans like it.

When to Use Your Repeating Ideas

You can repeat shows as often as you like. If they're on a particular day of the week, like Tropical Tuesday, you can do them every Tuesday, or you can wait a few weeks between uploading them. It's up to you!

The same goes for sounds effects, music, and other gags or jokes that you do in your videos. You don't need to do them in every video you make. You probably shouldn't. Or you should at least do them a little differently each time, if you do them in every video.

But most big YouTubers will use a "repeating thing" in one video, then make a few videos where they use *different* "repeating things," and then use the first "repeating thing" again in another video.

How to Come Up with Ideas

Since you learned about the "ten ideas" trick for brainstorming earlier, you're going to come up with things that you want to repeat. For example, if you have a channel about tabletop games, you might have a "show" where you and your friends play your favorite game. You might have a different "show" where you check out a new game that

The YouTube channel Geek & Sundry uploads videos where fun people play tabletop games. The channel also uploads a variety of other kinds of geeky videos.

you bought. You might have a third "show" where you make up new rules for existing games and try them out.

But a lot of your ideas, jokes, and repeating things will happen accidentally. In one video, you may hold up a picture of Iron Man with his mask open, and say "Tony Stark thinks this is a great idea." You can do that again in the next video if it's appropriate. Just make sure that your repeating ideas are easy to do. And have fun experimenting with them!

Notice how your favorite YouTubers use repeating things in their videos. You probably didn't even notice them before! They'll help you come up with ideas of your own.

TO BLOOPER OR
NOT TO BLOOPER

I like bloopers. I like it when my favorite YouTubers make a funny mistake and they keep it in the video. It shows that they're human, like you and me!

<aside>
YOUTUBE TALK

A "blooper" is a funny/ embarrassing error you make while shooting your video. Bloopers get laughs from your viewers.
</aside>

Should You Use Bloopers?

Most YouTubers don't include bloopers, but I don't think it's because they don't want to. They probably just say to themselves, "Oh, I messed up. I'd better cut that out of the final video."

But if you want to make your viewers laugh, include some bloopers.

Bloopers also make your viewers feel like they're seeing the "real you"! It's like a behind-the-scenes look at you. It's seeing you when you have your guard down. Viewers love that!

They don't want to just see someone who's perfect. Your videos can make you seem perfect, because you're cutting

*Me, falling out of my chair.
(And then laughing a whole lot on the floor!)*

out all the parts where you make mistakes. Viewers want to see someone who's mostly perfect *but* confident enough to include their embarrassing mistakes in their video.

It's like with your friends: you can mess up together, and it's hilarious.

What Qualifies as a Blooper?

If you accidentally knock something over while you're shooting, that's funny.

If someone walks into your room by mistake while you're shooting, and that messes up what you're saying, that's funny.

If you get completely tongue-tied while you're trying to say something normal, that's funny.

If you just start laughing because you make a mistake, that's funny. (Especially if you're trying to keep a straight face but you just can't!)

When to Show Bloopers in a Video

There are four places where you can show bloopers in a video.

First, you can start your video with a blooper. That can be your cold opening.

Second, you can include bloopers during your video. For example, you say, "And this is my wonderful dog, Angel! I love you so much, Angel!" but Angel turns and walks out of the room. Whoops! You can include that shot, then quickly cut to you hugging your dog Angel (to keep her in the room!) and saying, "This is my wonderful dog, Angel!"

Third, you can include them after your branded outro. Consider starting off (like some of the pros do) with a really funny blooper, then show some less-funny bloopers, then finish with your best blooper where you're completely cracking up because of some disaster.

> **PRO TIP:**
> When you show a blooper during a video, it's good to drop any background music you're playing. When you cut back to a shot that worked, start the background music again.

Fourth, you can do what D-Trix does and create a totally separate video for your bloopers! He uploads his main video that looks perfect, and then he uploads a second video with all his funny mistakes. It takes more time to do that, because you're editing a whole separate video, but then you get to upload two videos instead of one. Make sure to upload the bloopers video within twenty-four hours of uploading your main video so your fans still remember the main video. (You can even upload the blooper video right after the main video!)

COLLABORATIONS

Why It's Good to Collaborate with Friends

Two heads are better than one, right?

When you make a video with a friend, it's easier to come up with ideas and jokes because there are two of you. You'll probably be more comfortable on camera because you're just hanging out with a friend (which you normally do anyway!). You can just be yourself, and horse around, and have fun! And that looks great in a YouTube video!

Hannah and Kaylee (of the Hannah & Kaylee channel) do amazing collabs even though they don't upload videos very often. They sit in the front seat of their car in a parking lot and play these two characters with thick Louisiana accents who are pretending to teach you a life hack, like how to keep mosquitoes from biting you.

YOUTUBE TALK

When you make a video with another YouTuber, it's called a "collaboration". Most YouTubers shorten the word to "collab," as in, "Do you want to do a collab?" or "We should collab sometime!"

Their whole thing is to pretend they're being serious and educational while doing all kinds of physical humor, like covering their faces with nylon stockings to prevent mosquito bites. Their life hacks are ridiculous, they never plan them well enough before they start shooting (so everything goes wrong), and they end up laughing until they can't talk. It's fantastic!

Hannah and Kaylee in character at the start of a video.

Kaylee with a nylon stocking over her head (to "protect her from the mosquitoes") and Hannah cracking up.

Planning a Collab with a Nearby Friend

It's easiest to shoot a collab if your friend is in the same place you are (like Hannah and Kaylee in the car). If you're hanging out already, and you have a smartphone, you can just pick a topic, turn on your camera, and start talking about it or demonstrating it!

For example, you might be outside talking about how quirky one of your teachers is, and it seems like the perfect moment to make a video about the different kinds of teachers every student encounters. Just tap "record" and start talking!

If you plan ahead for your collab, agree to the time you'll shoot, where you want to shoot (your house? your friend's house? a park halfway between you?), maybe what you want to talk about, and the props you'll need (and who's going to bring what).

> **PRO TIP:**
> When you're thinking about collaborating with a friend, think about whether they're reliable. You don't want to prepare for an elaborate collab if they're not going to show up, or if they're going to forget half of the props you need!

When you get together for the collab you planned, make sure you're both in the right mood! If one of you is happy and the other one is angry about something, the video probably won't work. So make sure you're on the same page. Otherwise, it might be best to postpone the collab for another day.

Collabs with Other YouTubers

You're going to want to collaborate with other YouTubers you've seen too. But that's trickier. Luckily, there are some ways to make it more likely they'll want to collab with you.

Collab with Other YouTubers with Similar Sub Counts

You aren't going to be able to collab with Pewdiepie (who has 54, 163, 354 subscribers at the moment). For one thing, you probably can't reach him! He gets millions and squillions of comments and messages every day. He won't see yours.

Also, Pewdiepie wants to collab with other YouTubers who have millions of subscribers. You'll find that most YouTubers collaborate with other YouTubers who have similar subscriber counts. Take Tyler Oakley and Connor Franta for example: They both have over five million subscribers so it makes sense that they collab on YouTube.

Reach out to people who have similar sub counts as you. If you're just starting out, you can probably collaborate with other YouTubers who have fewer than five hundred subs. Different YouTubers you contact will have different attitudes about that.

The exception is for YouTubers with whom you already sort of have a relationship. If you've been leaving comments on a YouTuber's videos for months, and they reply to every one of them, and it seems like the two of you have a friendly relationship, then they might want to collab with you. They'll want to collab with you even more if you make it easy on them!

How to Make It Easy on Other YouTubers!

If you ask another YouTuber to collab with you, have a plan in mind first! Choose a topic. Know exactly what his or her part will be.

For example, you may say, "I'm doing a vid where I list things that I like to do when I'm bored. Could you make a quick video where you say five things that you do when you're bored? If you have time to actually do the activities on camera, that would be great, but even just saying them would help me out a lot!"

This is me as a pizzeria owner for a collaboration with Tommy Chaos.

I did a video collaboration last year where the guy asked me to pretend I was running a pizza shop. He was going to call in to order a pizza, and as the owner of the place I kept wanting to sell him more things. That was supposed to make him more and more frustrated. That YouTuber even sent me a script with some ideas of things to say. For me, that was easy to shoot! I put on a red shirt, and recorded a single shot of me picking up the phone, then offering more and more and more things for him to possibly buy: "Do you want stuffed crust? Gluten-free crust? Extra cheese? Okay, that's everything. Now, for desserts. Do you want our supreme brownie tray? Our basic brownie tray? Chocolate pizza dough bites?" It was a simple collaboration because he told me exactly what he wanted me to do! After I shot it, I just uploaded my unedited video to Dropbox and he did the rest.

Collab with Other YouTubers Whose Videos Are Similar to Yours

I did that collaboration with him because I like making funny videos, and he likes making funny videos. If he wanted me to talk about chemistry, or do a makeup tutorial, or discuss French poetry, I wouldn't have done it because those aren't my style and I know nothing about them.

So for a collab, pick other channels that make videos that are similar to yours. They don't have to be exactly the same, but there should be some overlap in your styles.

You'll need to make a few videos

PRO TIP:
Long-distance collabs are tricky. It may help to brainstorm ten different ways you can collaborate with someone who doesn't live in the same city as you. (And don't worry, none of the ideas has to be any good!)

before you ask another YouTuber to collab. If you ask someone to be in your video, but you don't have any videos yet, they won't be convinced you can even make a video! (And they don't know that you've read this book!) You need to show them you can make good videos, and show them what kind of videos you make.

Picking the Right Kind of Long-Distance Collab

Since you're in two different places, it's pretty hard to "play off" of each other. If they're shooting their part one day, and you're shooting your part another day, it's completely different than if you're shooting in the same room at the same time. When you're apart, you aren't making each other laugh or giving each other ideas and bouncing off each other in real time.

PRO TIP:

If you ask another YouTuber to collaborate with you, they're going to watch the videos you've uploaded so they can see what you're like. If someone asks you to collab, you should do the same!

This is not a problem in the example where they are listing five things they do when they're bored. You can just edit their video into the middle of your video.

But if you're trying to shoot a cut scene with them, or if the two of you are supposed to be having a conversation, that's tricky. You usually have to figure out a way for the scene to make sense when you're in two different places. For example, you could be on a phone call or a video chat. Or you could be "watching a video" of the other YouTuber; they shoot a video of exactly what you asked them to say, and then you make a video of yourself watching that video of theirs, and maybe commenting on it out loud.

A sock puppet video from Megan Sparks.

Another option, if you wanted to get really kooky, is to do a puppet show. You write out a script first, then you do the puppet show while being the voice for one of the characters. The other YouTuber records all the lines for the other character. When you get the video from them, you edit their voice into your video so it matches with the right puppet. (That's a lot of work, and it's kind of complicated, but it is an option!)

YouTube Collaboration Etiquette

Whatever kind of collab you do, make sure you do most of the work. The other person is a guest. They should have fun just being on camera (or recording their voice if you do the puppet thing).

That means you plan what's going to happen when you shoot. You come up with the topic for the video, and you write the script if you need to. You do all the editing. You upload the video to your own channel; don't insist that they upload it to their channel (unless they really want to!).

It's important to make friends around YouTube, because the more friends you have, the better your future on YouTube is going to be!

PART THREE:
PLANNING FOR THE FUTURE

BUILD YOUR (FAN) COMMUNITY

One of the best parts of making YouTube videos is knowing how many viewers you've reached and getting to interact with them. The more fun comments I get on my videos, the happier I am!

Fans love hearing from YouTubers too. When I leave a comment on a video and the creator replies to me, it's like I'm texting a friend and the friend is texting me back. That makes me want to watch all the videos from that creator, and to stay friends with them.

A lot of viewers thank me for making videos, and I love it!

What does that mean for you? Make your fans feel important! They will stay fans, they'll tell their friends how cool you are, and your channel will grow and grow!

Reply to Comments

I spend an hour or more every day replying to comments. (If I get more comments, I spend more time!) I like to reply to everybody. They cared enough to leave a comment on my video, so I should show them I'm grateful by replying. I always try to be upbeat, encouraging, helpful, and/or funny.

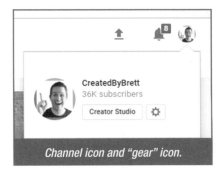

Channel icon and "gear" icon.

Since I get a lot of comments on my videos—even on really old videos I uploaded years ago—I use YouTube's email notifications to make sure I see all the comments. YouTube can send you an email

Gear menu.

Notifications menu.

every time you get a comment on a video. The email includes a link that will take you right to the comment in the video.

You can set that up from the YouTube website in a browser. Click on your channel icon in the upper right corner, then click on the "gear" icon. The "Gear Menu" will appear. On the left side, click on "Notifications". On the Notifications page, make sure you have the options selected that says, "Send me emails about my YouTube activity (except emails I've unsubscribed from)".

If you're getting a lot of comments on your videos, you can also visit YouTube.com/comments. That will show you all the comments on all

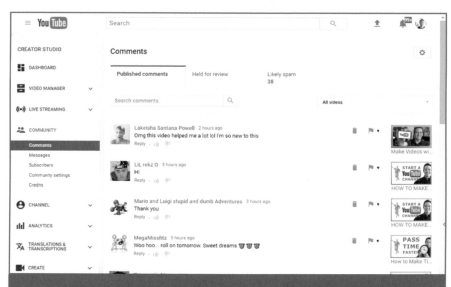

Youtube.com/comments shows you all your latest comments. The thumbnail images on the right side show you which video the comment was made on. The tabs at the top show comments that you need to review before they're visible to everyone. source: www.youtube.com/comments

your videos. The newest comments appear at the top. However, if a viewer replied to another comment, that won't appear at the top of the screen, and you might never see it. So be sure to check your email notifications too!

Involve Your Fans in Your Videos

Ask your fans what they want to see you make videos about! If you do product reviews, ask them what products they want to see. If you do makeup videos, ask them what looks they want to learn.

When you make a video that was suggested by a fan—or by a few fans—mention them in the video! Say, "YouTubeGirl_2345 asked me how to juggle. Well, YouTubeGirl_2345, I know how to juggle with two balls, and with three balls. I'm going to show you two-ball juggling first!" If you know how to show a picture of their comment on screen, with their channel name, your fans (especially YouTubeGirl_2345) will love it!

Give your viewers shout-outs. Thank them specifically (like YouTubeGirl_2345), and thank them generally, either at the beginning

When my fans ask questions and I use them in videos, I show their question on screen.

or end of your videos ("I make these videos for you. Without you watching them, I wouldn't have any reason to make my videos. So THANK YOU for watching and sharing and everything you do!").

Ask Your Fans to Like, Comment, and Subscribe

You might have noticed that I wrote, "Thank you for watching and sharing, and for everything you do." That subtly suggests to your fans that they should share your videos! If your fans share your videos, then more people see them, and more people will subscribe, and your channel will grow.

Most YouTubers (even the really big ones!) say something in their video like, "If you like this video, please like, comment, and subscribe." It works. Viewers are used to it. And it reminds them what to do. Ask your viewers to like, comment, subscribe, share, and tell their friends. Make it sound casual. Include it as part of your video outro. If you're nervous saying it, just say it a few times on video until it comes out

When I ask viewers to subscribe I like to show the word "Subscribe" on the screen.

sounding normal! Then just use the one good version (and cut out all the others).

Have a Schedule

Did you notice that a lot of popular YouTubers upload videos on particular days of the week? Some upload every Monday, Wednesday, and Friday. Some upload Tuesday and Friday. Some upload every Saturday.

Fans like to have a schedule! They like to know, "It's Thursday – time for another video from my favorite YouTuber!" You become part of their weekly routine. They look forward to seeing you on those days every week!

Upload at the same time of day, too (9:00 a.m. Pacific Standard Time used to be ideal, but this can change over time).

How to Handle Trolls

Unfortunately, there are trolls on YouTube. If you get a mean comment, don't reply. Your goal is to shut down the troll, so just block them from your channel and delete the comment. (YouTube might even delete the comment for you.)

The YouTube app and the website handle reporting differently. In fact, YouTube keeps changing the way they handle this. But the general idea is to click or tap on the three dots next to a user's comment, and select either "Report," "Block," "Hide User's Comments," or something like that.

You can also block them directly from the troll's channel. On the app, go to the person's channel, tap on the three dots in the upper right corner, and select "block". On the YouTube website, go to the channel, continue to their "About" tab, click on the flag icon with the triangle next to it, and select "Block user". After I do this, I go back to my video where the person left the comment, and I delete the comment too (by clicking on the three dots next to the comment).

PRO TIP:
Figure out what country most of your fans are probably in. Upload when they're awake, probably at the beginning of their day. Don't upload videos in the middle of the night!

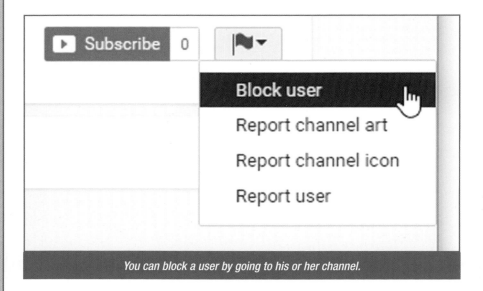

You can block a user by going to his or her channel.

BOOST YOUR YOUTUBE RANKING

There are few simple things you can do to make your videos appear higher in YouTube search. These might change over time, because YouTube keeps changing its search algorithm, but I'll share some solid suggestions that should help boost your ranking.

Stay Active

Create at least one video every week. YouTube likes to see channels that keep uploading new content.

This means that if you get really inspired one weekend and you shoot three videos, it might be a good idea to upload one right

> **YOUTUBE TALK**
> "Watch time" is the amount of time that a viewer stays on your channel, watching your videos.

away, then wait a week to upload video 2, then wait another week to upload video 3! There's nothing wrong with shooting videos ahead of time and then uploading them according to your regular upload schedule.

"Watch Time"

YouTube made up the term "watch time". It's the total amount of time that someone stays on your channel watching your videos.

For example, if someone watches a video of yours that's two minutes long, but then they watch another

> **PRO TIP:**
> "Top 5" or "top 10" videos are good for increased watch time, because viewers typically want to see all five or all ten of the examples you give!

video of yours that's five minutes long, the total watch time for your channel is seven minutes.

YouTube rewards channels with higher watch time. Videos from those channels appear higher in the YouTube search listing.

One way to boost your watch time is to make several videos that go together. For example, you could make a whole series of videos about

COMMUNITY ∨

CHANNEL ∨

ılıl ANALYTICS

Overview
Realtime

Revenue reports
Revenue
Transaction revenue
Ad rates

Watch time reports
Watch time
Audience retention
Demographics
Playback locations
Traffic sources
Devices
Live streaming
Translations [NEW]

Engagement reports
Subscribers

CreatedByBrett 🏳
Created: Nov 28, 2010 · Videos: 315
CHANNEL

Last 28 days (Feb 27, 2017 – Mar 26, 2017)

Watch time
Minutes

135,236 ▼

Views

69,502 ▼

Likes   Dislikes   Comments
1,003 ▲   152 ▲   204 ▼

This is the Analytics page for my CreatedByBrett channel. "Watch Time" is an option on the far left, about halfway between the red "Overview" option and the bottom. You can find your own Analytics at www.youtube.com/analytics?o=U.

how to get good grades in school. At the end of each one, you could say something like, "I hope you liked this video! Remember to watch the last video I made, where I show you my trick for studying so you really remember the information!"

PRO TIP:

You can include the link to a prior video in the description of your current video. Make sure to include the "http://" at the beginning of the link so viewers can click on it. Place that link towards the top of your description so viewers see it right away.

That will get your viewer to check out your last video! And if you say that at the end of every video in the series, they may watch every video!

EDIT METADATA FOR TENTPOLE EVENTS

Get More Views

When people hear about something new, they all go to YouTube and search for it. If there's a new viral video or big movie trailer that just came out, that viral video or movie trailer is going to get a lot of views in just a few days.

You can use this to get more views on your old videos!

Let's say you made a video where you're talking about how Rihanna gets ready to shoot a music video. The description and tags probably mention her *last* music video. To match all the current searches for her *new* music video, just update your title, description, and tags to include the title of her new song. It's easy, and it works!

> **PRO TIP:**
> You can update the metadata for any video of yours that becomes relevant again. When a trailer for a superhero movie sequel comes out, and you made a video for the first movie about that superhero, update your metadata. At the beginning of October, if you made a Halloween costume tutorial last year, update your metadata.

Just be sure your old video isn't *only* about her old song. Your video has to be generally about Rihanna and her process, or else people will click off of your video, which will make YouTube identify it as unpopular.

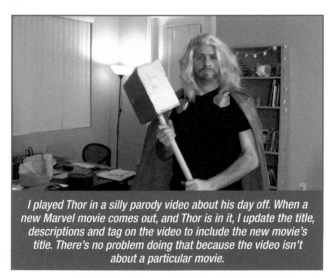

I played Thor in a silly parody video about his day off. When a new Marvel movie comes out, and Thor is in it, I update the title, descriptions and tag on the video to include the new movie's title. There's no problem doing that because the video isn't about a particular movie.

THE "DON'T" LIST

You're probably making videos that follow the rules, and you're probably using proper YouTube etiquette. But there are a few things you should avoid as a responsible YouTuber:

Don't Use Other People's Stuff

Don't use copyrighted material. That includes music videos, TV commercials, popular songs, pictures that you find online, etc. "Fair Use" is the only exception.

The Fair Use Doctrine is a part of United States law that lets you can use copyrighted songs, videos, etc. in some cases, but the rules are strict. You need to be using it for education, for making commentary on the source material, or for parody (making fun of the source material). However, if you do, there's a good chance that YouTube won't let you make any money off the video. The ad income will go to the person whose material you're using.

And even if you think your video is covered under Fair Use, the copyright owner can still tell YouTube to delete your video. If you protest (which YouTube allows you to do), the copyright owner can still sue you. That means you would need to defend yourself in court, which is expensive and takes months or years to resolve. Even if you win the case, it's not worth it.

So don't use copyrighted material.

Don't Be Too "Adult"

Around the end of 2016, YouTube changed its policies. If you swear much in your videos, YouTube won't let you make money from them. The same obviously applies to nudity and other "adult" content. It may prevent most users from viewing your video, and they may just remove the video altogether.

Don't Be Obnoxious in Comments

Don't spam on other videos. There are some low-level YouTubers who go onto popular videos and comment, "Watch my videos!" They think that people reading the comment will go to their channel and watch their videos to give them more views.

But it just comes across as selfish and irritating. Plus, the person who uploaded the video will probably delete the comment or mark it as spam. That gives your channel a bad reputation, so your videos show up lower in a YouTube search (or not at all!).

Don't Offer "Sub for Sub" in Comments

Don't leave a comment saying anything like, "Sub for sub! If you subscribe to my channel, I'll subscribe back to your channel, 100%, within twenty-four hours! Just leave me a comment saying you did!"

YouTube catches those comments automatically most of the time, and marks them as spam. That means people will never see them anyway, and YouTube will give your channel a bad reputation so people won't see your videos as often.

Don't Cheat on Your Videos' Metadata

It may also seem like a good idea to just list popular search terms in the description of your video. That would make your video appear higher in YouTube search, right?

It would, except YouTube is good at catching that, and they will delete your video.

If you keeping doing it on your videos, YouTube can delete your whole channel.

Also don't cheat on your video's thumbnail. It should either be a frame from the video, or it should represent the video overall. If you use a thumbnail that misrepresents

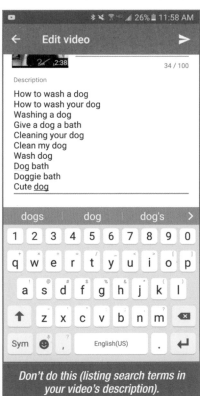

Don't do this (listing search terms in your video's description).

your video, other YouTubers will report it. That will lower your channel's reputation and YouTube will lower the search rank of all your videos, not just the one with the misleading thumbnail.

Report this video ×

What is the issue?*

◯ Sexual content ❷

◯ Violent or repulsive content ❷

◯ Hateful or abusive content ❷

◯ Harmful dangerous acts ❷

◯ Child abuse ❷

◯ Spam or misleading ❷

◯ Infringes my rights ❷

◯ Captions issue

Content that is massively posted or otherwise misleading in nature.

Flagged videos and users are reviewed by YouTube staff 24 hours a day, seven days a week to determine whether they violate Community Guidelines. Accounts are penalized for Community Guidelines violations, and serious or repeated violations can lead to account termination. Report a channel.

*Required   Submit

You can report a misleading thumbnail image. And a lot of YouTubers do.

CONGRATULATIONS!

Hopefully you've been making videos while reading this book! Your videos probably got better and better because you learned more and added more cool, advanced YouTube techniques. You might even have a growing number of subscribers!

Well, be sure to be nice to those subscribers. They like your videos, they like YOU, and they watch what you upload. Treat them well! Ask them what they want to see. When they compliment you in the comments section, thank them.

And if they have questions about how to make videos, especially how to make their FIRST video, give them advice. Start simple. You've learned a lot by reading this book, and you're pretty much a pro, but they're new to it. Give them some basic guidance, and maybe even watch one of their videos and provide some constructive feedback for them. ("Try putting the light in front of you instead of behind you." "I was distracted the whole video because your dog was in the corner and he was doing funny stuff! Next time, hold him and make the video together!")

Being creative is fun. And being creative in YouTube videos is A LOT of fun! Your viewers should get to have just as much fun as you do, so help them out!

And some day, who knows? You might even collaborate on a video together!

But regardless of what happens, YOU keep having fun making videos. I know I do!

Thanks for reading my book!

SOURCES

YouTube Image Sources

"I learned to play the guitar in 24 hours." YouTube video, 7:26. Posted by Luke Korns, March 22, 2017. http://www.youtube.com/watch?v=lTgdspqSKic.

"Best 6 year old Soccer player in the U.S." YouTube video, 3:26. Posted by Isaiah Izaguirre, June 25, 2015. http://www.youtube.com/watch?v=nB4WrPFhtns

"Tutorial makeup Korea untuk remaja [Daddoa]." YouTube video, 3:32. Posted by Owiena Tan, March 25, 2017. https://www.youtube.com/watch?v=EPx5V6-shNl.

"Baking with Mimi & Marbles" YouTube video, 3:34. Posted by jasonrip99, March 25, 2017. http://www.youtube.com/watch?v=oODGJe2FLY8.

"Amazing Claw Machine Win!!!" YouTube video, 3:23. Posted by Toby Turner, March 16, 2016. www.youtube.com/watch?v=zpkGm2GQjsc.

Flying Kittens channel, (no longer live) www.youtube.com/watch?v=S9hrLTlvMg0.

"Heart's Birthday Week! PT 3." YouTube video, 5:42. Posted by Arnold Telagaarta, March 10, 2017. www.youtube.com/watch?v=Gje8ascB3Tc.

"Cooking without pants." YouTube video, 12:40. Posted by Grace Helbig, August 10, 2017. www.youtube.com/watch?v=C0horKLDWrg.

Shane Dawson, (no longer live) www.youtube.com/watch?v=jLZjN5uSA2

"Ultimate Water Bottle Flip! (Dear Ryan)." YouTube video, 3:00. Posted by Ryan Higa, August 20, 2016. www.youtube.com/watch?v=YmY94vsb64U.

"The Rock's 14,000 Calorie Cheat Meal Challenge!" YouTube video, 8:28. Posted by theDOMINICshow, February 18, 2017. www.youtube.com/watch?v=Gl4Jt 8AWFY0.

"Will Wheaton's Tabletop Preview w/ Sean Plott Freddie Wong, Flaming Interns!" YouTube video, 1:11. Posted by Geek & Sundry. March 19, 2012 www.youtube.com/watch?v=kVKQ3VgGN3o.

"HoW to PrOtEcT YoUrSelF from MoSqUiToeS." YouTube video, 3:58. Posted by Hannah & Kaylee, June 18, 2014. www.youtube.com/watch?v=KqCBGrLcsA0.

"Como te llamas, como estas, cuantos anos tienes, que te gusta hacer." YouTube video, 0:38. Posted by Megan Sparks, March 28, 2017. www.youtube.com/watch?v=hA-DpPCQv3g.

Gielen, Matt. "Want to Know the Best Days and Times to Post YouTube Videos? Here's a Yearly Calendar." Posted on January 12, 2015. www.tubefilter.com/2015/01/12/best-days-times-to-post-youtube-videos-yearly-calendar/

Links to my YouTube videos (the ones referenced in this book):

"EXTREME FACE PALM—taking face palm to the next level." YouTube video, :50. Posted by AMillionViewsADay, November 1, 2015. www.youtube.com/watch?v =gy2m-gzRFOY.

"Who Said It Best Challenge - BigManTyrone and BrettFromLA." YouTube video, 2:13. Posted by BrettFromLA, November 14, 2014. www.youtube.com/watch?v=366nF8r3i5k.

"How to Choose Between Fans?!??!?" YouTube video, 3:32. Posted by AMillionViewsADay, May 6, 2016. www.youtube.com/watch?v=q3Nf7dlSbak

"YouTube Lighting Tips—Natural Light—Sunlight." YouTube video, 1:05. Posted by CreatedByBrett, December 9, 2016. www.youtube.com/watch?v=X9p88aSMymY.

"Make Videos with Your Phone (cell phone / mobile phone YouTube video tips!)" YouTube video, 5:01. Posted by CreatedByBrett, June 21, 2016. www.youtube.com/watch?v=OPda7mPdRsU

"NEW SCI-FI / FANTASY UNIVERSE!!!!! (how to create a universe out of toys & junk)." YouTube video: 3:43. Posted by AMillionViewsADay, January 24, 2016. www.youtube.com/watch?v=W0subpM32l4

"How to Brainstorm Ideas—The "10 Ideas" Technique." YouTube video: 4:58. Posted by CreatedByBrett. June 8, 2016. www.youtube.com/watch?v=bgndSmYPO78

"Only One Hand?? ("Quick Questions" Q & A Video - Questions and Answers!)" YouTube video, 4:44. Posted by AMillionViewsADay, July 4, 2016. www.youtube.com/watch?v=C0l1CQdty0I

"Thor: The Dark World PARODY—Thor's day off!" YouTube video, 1:59. Posted by Brettflix, November 7, 2013. www.youtube.com/watch?v=6_fulyHIPW4.

"Types of Parents," YouTube video, 11:28. Posted by IISuperwomanII, June 5, 2014. www.youtube.com/watch?v=wTIXFfpjf1o.

Useful Resources

YouTube app
YouTube.com
Velosofy.com
SoundJay.com
Gimp.org
Adobe Premiere CC
Final Cut Pro